"A wise and generous memoir, keenly observed, unflinchingly recorded, written with humor, empathy, and love. Nelson's coming of age—as a daughter, sister, wife, and mother herself—feels worthy and true."
DINAH LENNEY, AUTHOR OF *COFFEE*

"*This is How We Leave* is full of sweet and somber recollections of a family that is both happy and unhappy in its own way—as all families are. Nelson is a master of structural ingenuity, of suspense mitigated by calm meditation. Full of quiet, delectable detail— the heightened sounds and smells of bittersweet recollection—it is a book of conflicting emotions, of ambivalence and nostalgia, and a reminder that we come to know those we love the most by hearing and telling stories about them."
J.C. HALLMAN, AUTHOR OF *B & ME: A TRUE STORY OF LITERARY AROUSAL*

"Joanne Nelson welcomes us into her life like a good friend with coffee and crumb cake. *This Is How We Leave* offers wrenchingly human stories—about love and loss, abuse and abandonment, betrayal and redemption, traffic tickets and holiday rituals. Something in this writer's voice—a warmth, a wonder—won't let us turn away. Nelson is a keen observer: of her grandfather chewing tobacco at the kitchen table, of her own young comforts (feet 'warm and dry in my own bread-lined galoshes'). Nelson's life is filled with both necessary and chosen solitude—yet again and again she shows us the depth and meaning of human connection. This book abounds with honesty. Nelson is not afraid to eat a sandwich at her mother's deathbed; she is not afraid to tell us how she feels about it, then and after. The gift of these stories lies both in their integrity and in the irrefutable call to live a life of courage.
LISA C. KRUEGER, AUTHOR OF *RUN AWAY TO THE YARD*

About the Author

Joanne Nelson's writing appears in anthologies and literary journals such as *Brevity*, *The Citron Review*, *the museum of americana*, *Consequence*, and *Redivider*. In addition, she is a contributor to "Lake Effect" on WUWM—Milwaukee's NPR station. Nelson writes creative non-fiction, essays, poetry, and commentaries on craft. She lives in Hartland, Wisconsin, where she develops and leads community programs, maintains a psychotherapy practice, and adjuncts. Nelson holds an MFA from the Bennington Writing Seminars, an MSSW from the University of Wisconsin-Madison, and is a certified meditation instructor.

More information is available at
wakeupthewriterwithin.com

this is how we leave

joanne nelson

Vine Leaves Press
Melbourne, Vic, Australia

This is How We Leave
Copyright © 2020 Joanne Nelson
All rights reserved.

Print Edition
ISBN: 978-1-925965-36-0
Published by Vine Leaves Press 2020
Melbourne, Victoria, Australia

Cover design by Jessica Bell
Interior design by Amie McCracken

A catalogue record for this
book is available from the
NATIONAL LIBRARY OF AUSTRALIA   National Library of Australia

For Chris, Alex, and Sam.
The three who matter most.

Author's Note

Many of the names in *This Is How We Leave* have been changed to afford privacy to those involved. Other than that, this memoir is as true as the vagaries of memory, time, and experience allow. Any mistakes are my own.

In My Office

In my basement office I keep a framed picture of my brothers and me, circa 1967. The three of us stand behind a kitchen table that features a three-tiered birthday cake and Currier & Ives coffee cups centered on matching saucers—enough to indicate the presence of grandparents. The coffee looks freshly poured, an equal amount in each cup and no lipstick smudges on the rims. Burnt orange colored Melmac creamer and sugar bowls wait, forks are at the ready, and an ashtray rests just left of center. A black planter with gold filigree hangs on the far wall, and an ivy's forever-green leaves loop in tangles above Steven's head, the vines trailing down behind his back. The boys wear plaid shirts, buttoned high, although Bill's shirt is only half-tucked in his corduroys. A detail I'm surprised my father, with his sharp words and critical eye, let slide. I'm dressed in a white turtleneck. The collar is rolled down to prevent that choky feeling, and there's a shadow between the shirt and my neck that emphasizes my pale skin and long features. The sight of my close-cropped pixie cut, hideous in the days of long, folksinger hair, makes me want to reach into the photo, grab the little girl's hand, and run away with her.

Bill holds a fishing pole, the new reel silhouetted against the pastel wall. He looks happy. Clearly, this is his scene: the lit candles on the cake in the foreground are way too many for me, and Steven, looking grim, is positioned a shoulder behind Bill. I'm tucked in between them, one hand in Bill's, the other unseen behind a chair. Steven drapes his arm across me. My size suggests I'm about five, which would make Bill fourteen and Steven twelve. We stand close together and take our cues from those on the other side of the table, the adults waiting for just one decent shot without all that goofing around so they can eat before the coffee gets cold or the candles burn down the house.

Despite it being Bill's day, I try to claim the moment. My jaw juts forward and my contorted grin shows all my teeth. My eyes are crinkled shut as I lean towards the camera. I'm an irritant to the adults, and if I don't knock it off pretty quickly I'll end up crying in my bedroom. Only Bill's smile appears true and emanates beyond his face, through his tall body, and into the gift he holds. Soon he'll begin staying away from home for longer and longer periods of time—even the simple present of rod and reel a ticket to somewhere else. Steven's eyes are distant, his mouth a tight frown. His expression reflects either some parental cruelty tossed his way or bad shutter timing; he's already closing his mouth for the final S of "cheese," while Bill and I continue enjoying that long E. A metaphor really, Steven was often out of sync with the rest of us.

***

My office desk is littered with various parts of my life: a dusty stack of journals to reread, a renewal reminder from the state of Wisconsin about my social work license, handwritten pages about community classes I hope to teach. A laptop rests at the center of it all and a well-used and comfortably stained coffee warmer takes pride of place a bit to the side.

A whiteboard hangs above the desk. It's covered with computer logins, phone numbers, and papers stuck fast with magnets. Things I shouldn't forget. One scrap is about paying attention. The note has escaped my monthly purging of outdated to-do lists and inspirational quotes for over a year, earning its keep again today by sending me back to that photograph, back to wondering about Steven's arm draped over my shoulder.

Protection, I decide, continuing to want the story to be about me—not about a random positioning while Steven waited for the song to be sung and cake served. I realize this only after staring at the image for so long I begin to feel the brown ridges of the vinyl chair against my thumb and hear the cupboard door open as my mother reaches for milk glasses. Maybe he sought comfort in the feel of my thin shoulder, connection with the one person not likely to yell at him. Me as a stabilizing factor—forever the baby and a girl to boot, always a blessing after two boys. A foil between our parents and him, that third side of the triangle to shift the focus elsewhere. Me as a shield, the relatives telling my father: "You can't be hitting a girl like you do those boys."

I don't want to be the baby—even the photo spells

this out. I'm pulling away, while Steven tries to hold on. The weight of his arm is heavy on me. And as we grow into our adult lives, I'll join the chorus of voices wanting him to work more, drink less. Our age difference no longer important, our heights nearly the same, I'll encourage all manner of change, using every technique I learned in my social work classes. Yet, he'll remain the same sad boy in the picture and I'll forget, for a long time anyway, how much solace is given just by standing next to someone. Then, years down the road, protection no longer possible, I'll give a final gift of comfort when I hold Steven as he takes his loud, terrible last breaths, his long face skeletal, his belly swollen from a broken, alcoholic liver.

***

The shelves next to the office door are jammed with vertically and horizontally stacked books interspersed with mementos: snapshots of my daughters, a crystal jar of paperclips, unlit candles, more framed pictures. All evidence of who I am now. One photograph includes my father, his mother, my brothers, Bill's three kids, and me. I stand next to Steven and he rests his arm on our nephew's shoulders, his mouth in that same childhood oval, as if he again missed the signal to smile. Steven had yet to meet his third wife; I hadn't had children.

Those bookshelves hold the answer to why I'm down here: the manuscripts recounting stories of escape or return and the mementos that tell their own suspended, yet scripted tales. It's the dual perspective of the little girl held close by her brothers in a corner of the kitchen, safe behind glowing candles

and of the woman at her desk in a basement office—
the soft hum of the dryer in the background, pictures
of her family surrounding her—who just wants to
tell about it.

If Not for the Mess

After my father's parents moved from Milwaukee to a mobile home park in Union Grove, Wisconsin, my Grandma Dora permitted chewing tobacco only at the kitchen table or outside on their trailer's patio. My Grandpa Eli didn't often mess with her rules and appreciated the leniency allowed outdoors. Grandpa Eli's gob-spattered Folgers's coffee can remained under his lawn chair for days without getting emptied, and he could spit in the grass if he wanted—the brown stream arcing away through the space between his front teeth—provided that no neighbors were around. As much as I enjoyed spitting Kool-Aid on the lawn through my own wide-spaced teeth or playing outdoors with Grandpa Eli, I liked it best when we stayed inside. Just the three of us.

Indoors we followed the same pattern day after day: bacon for breakfast, chores, and letter writing afterwards. During lunch we watched the *News at Noon*, with careful attention paid to the *Dialing for Dollars* game at the end of the newscast. Once sure we hadn't won, Grandpa Eli got up, shut off the TV, returned to the table, and brought the tin of Copenhagen snuff out of his pocket. He packed the red and gold box by flipping it over and over between his thumb and third finger while snapping the side of the can with his index finger. If the package was new, he cut around the edge of the cardboard container and loosened the leaves with his jack knife. A fresh, damp smell rose as he moved the knife around, different from the pungent smell of cigarettes at my other grandparents' home. Next he pinched off a measure of the finely ground, moist tobacco and placed it carefully between his bottom lip and gum, using a finger to dust off any flakes remaining on his face.

***

Those tobacco tin memories with their flecks of clinging leaves came back to me not long ago, when I spent a few days at a retreat center—a break from family and phones and to-do lists. It surprised me, even frightened me a bit, to realize how much I liked the time alone. To reach the retreat center, I had driven several hours north from my home in Hartland to the rural community of Denmark, Wisconsin.

Dairy farms border the roads I walked late each afternoon. Tractors and pickup trucks passed me when the sun began to sink. Each driver nodded and lifted his fingers off of the wheel in greeting. No head turns or smiles, just that hand half-raised from the wheel and the slow dip of the head. In the truck cabs, I'd see a gas station coffee mug jammed between dashboard and windshield, and more often than not a can of Copenhagen slipping its way down the dash.

Chewing tobacco is a solitary business. Grandpa Eli, with me sitting right next to him and Grandma Dora clearing the table, drew in on himself as he worked that chaw. He'd look down, elbows on his knees, hands folded together, and drum his black Oxford shoes: heel, heel, opposite toe, toe. He'd watch his shoes as if they moved on their own, the thin laces tied in careful, uniform bows, and his gray, everyday pants freshly ironed. As if this was his method of getting away, of claiming a space for himself.

There's a connection here. Grandpa Eli in his mobile home chewing tobacco and me, many years down the road, far from family and content to be alone. There's even a connection with those men in the pickups heading to or away. As much as I enjoyed the solitude, I knew I'd return home to the noise of a husband and kids. Growing up, that wasn't necessarily a given.

***

Grandpa Eli's father, Andrew, headed off on a sales trip one day around 1932 and never came back. Some forty years later, shortly before I turned twelve, my father called in sick to work one morning and then ran away. He, at least, left a note.

Tilted forward in my retreat room's one chair, arms folded on the small table I'd converted into a desk, I stared out my window across muddy cornfields too wet for walking. The days became a slow routine. For hours I mulled the meaning of my grandfather, his tobacco secure under his gum, watching those oxford shoes with their harmless miles of heel, heel, toe, toe. What kept him sheltered in that kitchen or content on the patio? What made it likely I'd return home? Didn't we both taste the desire to find a different life? Lives led without spouses or children and all of the demands that came with mortgages and PTA membership. Day after day of endless sunny relationships, forever dwelling in some fantasy California life filled with warmth and ease.

Sometimes I walked on a path near the fields, the previous year's cornstalks still littering the ground, geese hiding among hillocks or resting in puddles leftover from the wet spring weather. A fresh, earthy smell perfumed the air and returning birdsong filled the days. Still, even in this restful place, I worried about my arguing daughters and a dozen other things. I thought about all I had dreamed of, all I'd wanted to become. Looking across the land, despite the mud and the mist, I willed myself to see my long-dead grandfather and the childhood me appear, each posed to offer a message, some clear reason to stay.

***

I loved sitting at the maple laminate kitchen table with Grandpa Eli. On occasion he'd let me hold a freshly opened container of Copenhagen. The moist scent of the damp, smoky leaves all the stronger once I dipped my fingers in and disturbed his careful packing. Grandma Dora, bringing a game or her sewing to the table, would shake her head. "Eli, she gets it all over the place."

"No I won't," I'd answer while he placed the lid on the can and put it away in his shirt pocket, tapping his hand against its hidden weight over his heart.

"You're getting me in trouble now," his only reply.

My grandmother was right. No matter how carefully I shook my fingers over the container, tobacco wound up on the floor and in my clothing and made my hands smell for hours. The rich tobacco tang surprised me whenever I put a hand to my face—not pleasant exactly, but not bad either. I imagined one day I'd try tasting a bit when no one was looking.

I liked having Grandpa Eli near us, although it was Grandma Dora who mostly entertained and cared for me. She kept me busy in the afternoons, letting me knit with her extra yarn while she made dresses for my Barbie dolls or started supper. Grandma Dora was the one to go to with worries or hurts, with broken dolls, or scraped knees, and Grandpa Eli was the one to fix bikes and roller skates or get the Mercurochrome and Band-Aids out of the bathroom cabinet. I picture him with his head bent over some task, his thick, dark hair oiled back and parted on the right. The tap of his shoes between the clicks of my slow needles and the occasional expulsion of his chew became a rhythmic background to our long afternoons in the safe cocoon of the trailer.

Spit—his need to—was why Grandpa Eli could dip only in designated areas. When inside, he hocked into the Folgers coffee can kept under the kitchen table, near his chair leg. I stayed clear, not willing to risk seeing the brown slop or, worse, knocking the can over. The tobacco he favored came in a colorful box with a gilded-tin lid, the middle a warm burnished red with raised letters highlighted in black—the "o" of Copenhagen snuggled into the capital "C," giving a warm and inviting look. But when Grandpa Eli put the pinch of snuff into his mouth and the tin back in the front pocket of his button-down shirt, I avoided looking at him. I dreaded seeing the flakes covering his tongue, stuck to his teeth, or resting in the corners of his lips after he spat and wiped his mouth with a handkerchief. I wonder what Grandma Dora thought when she looked at him. If the grains clung to the inside of his lips, or if they transferred to her mouth when they kissed. Did she ever ask him to give it up or back away from his tobacco breath and the specks of chew clinging to his gums and teeth?

Grandma Dora dumped the contents of that coffee can down the drain at the end of the day—the tobacco gob mixed up with bits of bread and meat—rinsed the can and turned it over on the drain board to dry. Then she went to bed. It must have been years before her stomach stopped souring at the sight. She never complained or made a face; I suppose this became part of their balance, the rituals they'd developed as a couple, as lovers making a life, figuring out their own exchanges.

***

The year I turned six my grandparents moved from their red brick ranch house to the mobile home park with its shining, white-sided trailers, well-tended yards, and in-ground swimming pool. Their new place was down back roads in the township of Union Grove, an hour from us, and even further from where my grandmother's friends lived. Grandpa Eli said they were moving because he wanted to live in the country and not have such a big yard to mow. Grandma Dora, out of earshot, said he picked the spot so she'd be home more instead of chasing to her women's groups—her hen clubs. Years later my brother added a third layer, saying he heard Grandpa Eli moved to get away from our mother's meddling, hoping long-distance costs might prevent any but emergency telephoning.

I visited my grandparents as often as possible— long weekends and school holidays, entire weeks in the summer. I learned to swim in the trailer court's small pool. Grandpa Eli watched my every move and applauded each time I jumped off the diving board and dog paddled to the metal ladder at the deep end. If I looked over my shoulder when I climbed out, I'd see him turn his head to spit across the fence where he waited. My grandmother, I knew, wouldn't want him chewing in public, but I didn't tell. The sharp aroma of chlorine clung to me those summer days, even my pillow smelling of swimming the next morning.

One afternoon at a nearby park, Grandpa Eli wanted me to walk along the top of the split rail wooden fence separating the blacktop path from the woods. I feared falling and hesitated. He climbed up and demonstrated how easy it was to hold your hands out, place a foot down solid on the fence, move the other foot through the air and then repeat. Finally, out of fear that if I didn't try he'd continue, fall, and I'd get blamed for his death, I scrambled up to the top rail, spread my arms out wide, and learned to balance.

After I walked the length of two rails I lowered myself down, more anxious than proud. Grandpa Eli took my hand, swung it high in the air and said, "At home you can tell your Grandma what you did."

I nodded and skipped ahead, slowing when I thought of how Grandma Dora would look at him and say, "Her mother won't like that."

Mostly our days were predictable. Quiet stretches of games or crafts followed by supper and dishes—Grandpa and I helping to dry—then TV or cards, stories, and bed. Every evening Grandpa Eli took the knife and wallet from his pants pocket, along with the snuff and Black Jack gum from his front shirt pocket, and put them on top of his dresser.

I slept in my own room at the far end of their trailer and could hear them give each other a goodnight kiss, call a final "sleep tight" to me, and talk in low voices as I drifted off. Mornings I woke up to Folgers coffee percolating and bacon sizzling. The smells and sounds led me back down the hallway. Grandpa Eli was often still in his room, standing at the dresser, reversing the process of the night before: arranging all his possessions in the pockets of clean clothes in the exact same way.

The tobacco, gum, and jack knife were Grandpa Eli's talismans—like the stuffed monkey Grandma Dora had made me and that I slept with every night. Amulets to ground him and keep him safe from running off as his own father had. Just as our afternoons in the kitchen together became another kind of charm. Grandpa Eli rocking his feet, all those miles of heel, heel, toe, toe, without leaving his chair at the table, everyone safe and accounted for.

***

Some days Grandpa Eli took me for hikes in the woods or farm fields adjacent to the trailer court. Although I thought of him as old, he was agile enough to walk the uneven fields, stepping over clods of dirt, and picking his way through rows of the previous year's remaining cornstalks—both of us kicking up the smells of new earth, warm in the spring sun, me holding his rough hand.

Sometimes he'd bring a paper kite—the crossbow made of thin balsa wood—and string purchased at Woolworth's and wrapped around an orange juice can covered in duct tape. I'd run with the kite while he held the string. When he felt the wind's lift and pull, he'd yell, "Let go," and with my hand high above my head, I'd release the kite to let it catch the wind and rise. After the kite rose higher than the trees, he'd hand me the can and remind me to hold the edges and let the string out, bit by bit. One time, the wind tugged hard and I let go, sending the can bouncing over the field, the gust pulling the kite away from us, but not strong enough to lift the can into the air.

Grandpa Eli dashed after it with me in pursuit. The dusty hot smell of the soil got in my nose and I coughed as I hurried, not wanting to lose him. I didn't know Grandpa Eli could run, hadn't ever seen him do more than stroll, and I worried as I watched his legs in those everyday pants jumping over the rows, avoiding the brown withered stalks of corn. The clods of dirt sprayed dust from under his dirty shoes and even from the old can as it bounced along— the string impossible to see but still attached to the triangle of white high above us. If something terrible happened, if Grandpa Eli fell, or the kite and string flew away, I'd be blamed, yelled at, feel guilty forever. My grandparents wouldn't like me anymore or ever let me visit again.

***

At home there were older brothers to contend with and my mother's nervous spells—no way to know when I might spill or say something that sent her hunting for her pills. My father was loud and angry, given to calling us names and quick to slap. His worst behavior showed up at the dinner table, his workday frustrations still too raw for the neediness of a clamoring family. We couldn't anticipate what triggered him to yell or to strike out, but waiting for that moment made my stomach clench and the food go down in dry, sharp points.

I sat to my father's left during supper. Each night I'd move as far from him as the chair seat would allow, but my brother Steven was older and no longer able to wiggle around as I did. He sat to Dad's right, closest to his hitting arm, and got most of the smacks upside his head. Such sudden things, "Just shut up now" or "Don't talk so stupid," if dad didn't like our conversation. Then, silence. Only the sounds of forks scraping against plates, meat quickly cut, milk glasses carefully set down for the rest of the meal. Nobody asked for seconds.

***

I was a tummy-achy, cry-baby kind of kid—especially after visits to my grandparents. Grandma Dora once told me Grandpa didn't think my parents would want to bring me anymore if I kept crying. Though it seemed a convoluted way to tell me to stop, I got the message. I quit blubbering. The stomachaches got worse, and sitting on the toilet at home, listening to Dad yell at my brother for being lazy, or talk about me to my mom ("What the hell's wrong with her now?"), I wondered how Grandpa Eli could create such a horrible man.

My father, it appeared, favored Great-Grandpa Andrew—in temperament as well as in a desire to leave. Andrew had owned a small farm and worked as a traveling magazine salesman, leaving Grandpa Eli and his brother, Gus, to do most of the fieldwork. Andrew was critical and showed little appreciation for the work his boys did. Gus quit the farm fields of Zumbrota, Minnesota, for the city of Milwaukee as soon as he had enough money. Eli followed when Gus assured him of a job.

Years went by; my grandparents married, they had a son, and the past arguments with Andrew were history—if not forgotten and forgiven. Then, at the age of fifty-six, just a few years older than I am now, Andrew also drove away from Zumbrota. He left a wife, Julie, and an adopted niece, twelve-year-old Stirlee, to figure it all out. They did the expected things; police and neighbors searched everywhere, but there was never a clue to follow and never a sighting of him or his truck again. None of this was a secret, but by time I came along and grew old enough to want to solve the mystery, there didn't seem to be much interest. When I asked questions, Grandpa Eli would suck his teeth, look down at his hands, and say, "Nobody ever knew anything else, I guess." Grandma Dora was willing to speculate about all of the possibilities with me—including the rumor of an entirely different family in California—but even she couldn't say how anyone had felt at the time.

My grandfather couldn't have done much when the call about Andrew's disappearance came. He needed to work, the Depression lingered, and he had his own wife and child. There would have been no point to traveling the 300 miles back home from Milwaukee. I imagine the weight of the news on his life in those first days and years to follow as time kept passing without any information. At first, Grandpa Eli may have looked for his father to show up in Milwaukee, following the pattern he and Gus had set. Maybe he walked down streets, startling when a man coming out of a store or turning around a corner looked like his dad. I put myself inside my grandfather and envisioned how his heart pounded when he saw a certain tilt of a cap, heard a similar-sounding voice, or caught some scent—a cigarette or after-shave—that seemed familiar. After a few years, the loss likely settled into a hard spot in his chest, the memories picked apart only on birthdays or empty holidays.

Maybe Grandpa Eli envied Andrew on certain days. Days when he also wanted to run away from the responsibilities of being a grown-up. Occasions when, like me, he wondered about a different life and wished he had the guts to strike out on his own, consequences be damned.

I doubt it, actually. I'm guessing anytime Grandpa Eli considered leaving, he remembered the sound of his mother's voice telling him that her husband had gone missing, the interviews with police officers trying to track down Andrew, and the constant questions from relatives. To leave, knowing firsthand the toll on the abandoned family, would be too much to consider for more time than it took to dip his snuff and work the numbing shreds of tobacco into their spot. Something his son—shielded from the depth of the mess, the way we protect our children from the worst of our lives—didn't take into account.

***

Grandma Dora, who outlived Grandpa Eli by over twenty years, eventually gave me all of her stories. Hours of Sunday meals together when I learned everything she had left to tell, until there came a time when each story she told was one I'd heard before.

Grandma Dora only had a single incident to share when I asked what made my father mean and what Grandpa Eli—in my childhood eyes a near-perfect grandfather—had been like as a dad. She told me about a phone call home my father made when he served in the Army, before he got my mother pregnant and went AWOL to marry her. He talked about being lonely and began to cry. Grandma Dora became upset. Grandpa Eli told his son not to talk like that ever again. And he never did.

My grandfather didn't like Grandma Dora being unhappy. If my father—far away and alone— kept quiet, no one needed to feel anything. I can't remember enough of the story to know if Grandpa Eli delivered this message, the long-distance connection crackling and delayed as he said the words, or if my grandmother relayed his wishes. The latter was their usual style of communication—Dora informed people what Eli felt, decided, decreed. And when anyone asked Dora a question, she answered with, "Well, I guess Eli would say ..."

Grandpa Eli kept his feelings safe between his gum and lip, letting his wife deliver the messages. Grandma Dora kept herself safe as well—attributing all to Eli, never fully possessing an opinion or emotion of her own.

***

I don't remember if Grandpa Eli saved the kite that day in the field when he ran so fast, the dusty soil heavy in my throat as I followed. My recollection extends only to the chase and the vastness of the field and the sky. Despite my fears, my visits didn't end until I was twelve. That's when my own father ran away.

My mom and I spotted the note on his dresser at the same moment, held firm by a bottle of barely used cologne I'd given him for Christmas. The lonely penciled sentence, "I can't take it anymore," scribbled across a piece of paper torn from a notebook. The paper held in place with a woodsy oak scent, waiting for someone to find it, read the words, and then read them again.

She studied his note obsessively that first night, sharing it with neighbors and relatives, dissecting each word, the paper employed for their composition, the pencil used. My father called from a racetrack in Texas within a day or so. He returned home to us in Wisconsin a week after he'd disappeared.

The damage couldn't be undone. The Pandora's box of everything wrong with our family burst open. It seemed my father had made a trial run and now understood leaving was possible. The world went on and no lightning struck. Within weeks, he'd left for good and my mother extended her rage towards my grandparents, assuming they had known his plans. She didn't understand that lonesome call made from the army years earlier, the experience that kept her husband from sharing anything more.

***

I wonder about those days for Grandpa Eli, watching his son repeat his own father's worst sin. No longer far away or busy with work and a new baby, he had to witness the pain play out close to home with his own grandchildren—still unable to help, this time because of my mother's anger. I imagine him in his chair at the kitchen table, TV off, looking down at his shoes. Chaw tucked in its spot, the nicotine moving through his system, his awareness of the usual hit dulled as he tapped out his stay-in-place rhythm—pondering why he existed between these two men and what he'd done wrong.

Maybe he even wondered if the wrong thing had been sticking around to bear witness. He'd sought to avoid attention all his life. Grandma Dora told me he burned all the letters they'd ever sent each other; he didn't want people coming across them, reading all of their private business, and making judgments. Now here he sat, the one who stayed, the one having to answer all of the questions.

For Grandpa Eli, the worst thing would have been being alone with no wife to smooth the way, to tell everyone what he thought, or what he wanted to happen, or to rinse away his messes. Before long, just like before, I suppose he got busy with some project and began to bind each day to the next—continuing the routines of coffee after lunch, a dip of chew, some task to complete for his wife. And at the end of the day, emptying his pockets onto the dresser, everything safe in its spot until morning.

Alley Days

Back in the day, shoveling snow was a collective effort on Milwaukee's south side. The neighbors—the men and boys anyway—met in the alley dividing our block as soon as the flakes slowed. Looking back, I want to script this as a musical. Some dance number in the story of my life complete with twirling shovels, dancing dads in heavy coats, and a hand-jive section of mittened moms. But that kind of silliness didn't occur to us in the late 1960s, not on my block. No, the job was focus enough, any conversation reduced to weather observations or commentary on who wasn't outside helping.

My father and older brothers were always first out the door when the snow fell. Bill, the eldest, with his aura of adolescent anger and powerful long-lasting silences, was an energetic worker—his desire to be back in his room with his door closed making him fast and efficient. Steven plodded along knowing just how to irritate our dad, stopping to toss snowballs or to lean against his shovel and daydream. Dad kept moving, rapid and thorough, pausing only to greet a neighbor or holler at Steven: "What the hell are you doing? Get moving, now!"

The rising snow bank between the strip of sidewalk running from our garage to the house and the neighbor's bushes—the garage too close to the sidewalk on the other side to allow for any accumulation—became my kingdom. A princess overlooking her estate, I guarded the growing mountain or sat bundled on my Flexible Flyer sled, willing a brother to take me to Lyon's Park only one street over. I must have looked like a pine tree growing out of the hill, dressed in a cousin's cast-off green jacket with a fur-trimmed hood tied tight under my chin.

Back then, I believed the luckiest thing ever was having an alley behind the house—all the moms and kids passing back and forth between trips to the store or doctor and any other errands. My clear view in each direction allowed me to see if my friends or their annoying siblings were outside and ready to play. Always there was the call and response, the song of the nonexistent musical: *Can you play? Ask your Mom. What did she say?* Or the adults with their winter chorus: *Can you believe this? Sure is heavy.* Their words broken up by the metallic scrapes, the push and lift of shovels. Each scoop of snow a separate thought about those left in the house, events from the evening before, or visions of the coffee or Pabst waiting inside—an adult reward for completed work.

It wasn't all good from my snowy perch. I remember turning toward the house crying because the boys yelled at me for kicking snow back into the driveway, and then my relief at seeing Mom watching me from the kitchen window, one hand on the glass, the other holding the curtain back. She greeted me at the door with a scolding: "Get back out there and play." Did I think I could get her kitchen all wet just to go out again every ten minutes?

Sometimes my mother joined us. We were not one of those families that believed women shouldn't shovel or mow the lawn. Mom excelled at the detail work after everyone else tired, although occasionally she joined my dad for the heavy stuff. This always ended with him yelling about how she did everything wrong. I'd begin to shiver, my spot on the hill now cold, and beg to be carried away from the dirge-like wind to the comfort of hot chocolate and my Little House books. It was best if Mom waited until everyone except me had gone inside to warm up. Then, wrapped in Dad's heaviest coat, a kerchief on her head, and see-through boots pulled on over her shoes, she tidied up all the spots left undone. I trailed behind her and stomped leftover slushy spots into smithereens, my feet warm and dry in my own bread-wrapper-lined galoshes.

My mother's favorite time was in early spring when warm days created a river of snowmelt but ice remained thick around the alley sewer. Mom became queen of the block then. She attacked the ice with her trusty chopper, tongue out between her teeth, her arms bringing the blade down again and again until the ice gave way. The runoff flowed free, and the neighborhood was saved. Down the sewer grate all of that liquid swirled through pipes leading far away from us, past other neighborhoods, and into the rest of the city. To places, I imagined, where other little girls played lonely games while their moms chopped ice—long after the men and boys had left the stage.

The Occasional Wallop

My mother used to hit me with her shoes. Mostly she clobbered me in grocery stores, using the low pumps she favored for everyday wear underneath her slacks. I've retained more about the footwear, and the determined person who wore them, than the actual hitting. In my memory she reaches with long fingers toward her shoe, bending her leg—the left I think—from the knee back and up towards her outstretched hand. I look away from the powerful shoe to where her right hand grips a grocery cart; she steadies herself as she shifts for balance. A familiar expression dims her face: her eyes turned inward, her tongue between her teeth and peeking out the side of her mouth.

This was my mother's signature look indicating deep concentration. She used it when waxing the floor (sitting back on her heels to check for streaks), when placing pots of boiling water into the freezer to melt the accumulated ice, and before responding to any of my father's questions. "Got that tongue hanging out?" he teased if she took a long time to answer.

I was little, not even in school yet, when she started hitting me. Old enough to understand the meaning of her reach for the shoe, to back up and plead for mercy. Yet, young enough to cry and wrap my arms around her after she smacked me, to want comfort from her, to hide my naughtiness inside her arms.

The two of us spent all our time together. My brothers were much older, in middle school already, and my dad worked covering pipes for the Milwaukee schools. Mom did data entry for a local business one evening a week. Other than that and her psychiatrist appointments, we spent all our time together— day after day of house cleaning, soap operas, and supper preparation. We ran errands to the pharmacy or went shopping to break the routine. Trips to the grocery store were the best, despite the occasional wallop.

After we parked, I'd run ahead through the supermarket lot to swing on the railing separating the *in* door from the *out* door. I could do somersaults around the railing if I watched out for customers. Next, I jumped on the thick black mat in front of the *in* door, making the door swing open with a whoosh, until the manager hollered at me, "Move before you break the thing." I liked riding in the big grocery carts, surrounding myself with cans of vegetables and bright boxes of cereal like castle walls, the earthy smell of the week's bag of potatoes floating up from its spot near my feet. Even better was standing on the rounded bar at the front of the cart, leaning backwards into the air of the store while Mom pushed, shelves of crackers and cookies speeding past, the thin metal trim digging into my hands, my nails biting into my palms as I hung on. "Faster," I'd plead, until Mom tired of me and yelled that I needed to get off, I was too heavy. That I should, "Walk nice now. Like a big girl."

At the checkout the black conveyor belt rolled the groceries to the cashier who rang everything up while Mom looked through the coupons she'd pulled from an envelope in her purse. I liked to let my hand graze the belt, feeling the warmth from the friction against my skin. If I pushed down too hard the belt stalled until Mom snatched my hand away—a look of apology to the cashier—and squeezed my wrist such that red marks lingered long afterwards.

I watched for cans to get stuck and go bumping and bumping against the metal housing at the end of the roller, the label spinning past and colors swirling until the cashier picked it up and looked for the price tag stamped on it. I hoped some skinny item—a toothbrush or too-thin cellophane package— would pass between the roller and the housing, drop down to a depth impossible to reach with human hands, and cause a ruckus between the cashier and my mother—both women looking around for a manager to hurry over with the keys and open the cabinet under the belt. Once we paid and the bagged groceries were returned to the cart, we collected our Green Stamps—double if it was a Tuesday. At home, once everything had been put away and the paper bags folded and stored, we took the stamp book out of its drawer. I licked the minty backs of the stamps and covered the rows Mom pointed out.

***

My parents never bought me candy at the check-out. Luckily, opened boxes of Bazooka gum sat next to the register and I always happily took a few pieces; the dusty pink gum warm and soft in my mouth while I looked over the comic it came wrapped in. My two favorite activities, chewing gum and reading, for the quiet ride home. Some of the words I could make out on my own, the rest I saved for when Dad came home and sat with me, pointing out frame-by-frame what happened to Bazooka Joe and his friends, Mort and Jane. Then he read me my fortune: "Bazooka Joe wants me in his company," "I'm the top of everybody's list," and "Nobody does it better than me."

So much could come true for me if I continued to chew Joe's gum! I wanted to save up for a black eye patch and blue baseball cap—but girls didn't wear such things. When I pulled turtleneck shirts up over my face to look like Mort, Mom complained I wrecked the necks. Dad said, "Knock it off" or there'd be no more comics.

***

Part of me loved trips to the store, the time alone with my mother undivided by house cleaning or the demands of my father and older brothers. The two of us worked through our list and checked off each item after carefully comparing brands and weighing costs. Each week, Mom wondered if Kohl's, the grocery store down the road, might have lettuce cheaper. Her tongue peeked out when she perused the meat. From my spot balanced on the front of the cart, I mimicked her—gingerly placing my tongue between both incisors and my front teeth, letting the tip of it hang out. Biting my tongue didn't help me concentrate; I still had no clue about the advantage of pork over beef for our evening meal. But the pressure made me feel comfortable and solid somehow. I thought of the big girls who jumped rope in the alley behind our house, how they squeezed themselves if something good happened. I wondered if this tongue thing was similar, like a pinch to grow an inch on your birthday.

Another part of me felt my stomach tighten with the call to find my shoes, put on a jacket, and get in the car. I was an anxious child and agonized about doing wrong. At home, especially with my brothers in school, there were fewer opportunities to mess up. As long as I didn't step on a wet floor, break a glass, or let my grandmother know how much my mother napped, I avoided trouble. In the store, I worried I'd knock over displays of cans arranged in pyramids or make someone fall by tripping into them. The dread of making someone stumble loomed large in my mind, although I don't believe it ever happened. My most realistic fear in those days concerned getting hit—disappointing my mother and forcing her to strike me.

I never remembered any wrongdoing, thus no learning curve existed to suggest improvement over time. Most likely I whined or begged for some item, unbalanced the cart too many times, touched too many things, lagged behind, sassed back. Those all sound like my modus operandi, but it's all guesswork. Only her bent leg and the hand reaching for the shoe remain firm in my mind, the outlines solid and all the colors drawn in.

***

She didn't hit hard. The surprise and embarrassment hurt though—the combination of shock and sting hitting my neural pathways and butt simultaneously. I hated making my overwhelmed mother hit me. Sometimes my behavior upset her so much that she needed to call my grandmother and tell her, "Joanne acted so bad at the store I had to have a pill when I got home." Getting hit was better than making my mother swallow a pill, although they seemed to go together, as if the action of taking off her shoe coexisted with removing the lid from the mysterious medication bottle.

The key is how much I believed those shoe spankings were my fault, my actions controlling the hand and the poor brown pump forced to strike me. Until one day, while shopping, when we ran into an old friend of my mother's, someone she hadn't seen for a long time. The old friend had a daughter about my age and we began to play, running between the rows of baking supplies and noodles and seeing who could slide the farthest on their knees down the long, clean aisles. Both adults gave us looks, but we ignored them and grew bolder until the call rang out: "Don't make me take off my shoe." The warning was clear enough to quiet me. I stayed close but out of reach while the conversation continued. I heard my mother say, "It's easier than yelling. I reach down to my shoe and she straightens right up." They snickered together and the friend replied that maybe she'd try heels.

I froze. I stood reasoning this out: the other girl, now taking cookie packages from the shelf and putting them in her mother's cart, no longer interested me.

My ears buzzed and everyone seemed large, but far off—like being under water. Mom's world didn't just revolve around being with me; apparently, I existed to be mastered and tricked. Not only was this intervention a plan, it was an anecdote she could laugh about, a story to share with others.

I tried to glare at her, but she faced away from me, her head nodding as the other mom revealed some foolish thing her own child had attempted. A scene bubbled up in my mind from the weekend before. My parents had been talking in the kitchen, sitting at the table while I played on the floor with my Barbies. When the subject of my brother's falling grades came up, their voices rose and grew sharp. Mom reached down to her shoe, and I'd jumped and run to the hallway calling, "I didn't do anything." She startled at my sudden movement, then chuckled and said, "I'm just scratching my foot." Dad shook his head at me, told me to clean up my dolls, and they changed the subject.

I never wanted to see Mom's friend again. She had a nasty laugh, and I hated her. Her little girl acted like a brat, and I scowled at her from where I stood near the adults.

Walking to the car after we checked out, chewing my gum, another Bazooka square in my hand for the car ride, I did my best to scrape the tops of my shoes with each step—something expressly forbidden.

Realizing that more variables influenced spankings than disobedience was a game changer. My bad behavior had been acceptable to me and seemed as fleeting as my good behavior. Discovering my mother thought about how to harm me struck a different blow. I'd assumed her actions flowed from each moment—the same as mine. I didn't understand how to label anger or how my mother's prescriptions fit into this. I *did* know the hot way my face felt meant shame—like the time a neighbor had caught me pulling down my pants to pee in our front yard.

***

There were more surprises to come. Not long after that shopping trip my mother saw me pocket gum from the box on the counter. When we left the store she ranted, told me the police could arrest me for stealing, and used her shoe to smack me across the butt while we stood in the parking lot. I was confused. I thought children could have the gum, just like the lollipops freely handed out at the bank or beer depot. Mom refused to listen or explain and sent me to my room once we got home so she could take a pill and lie down.

I wonder what this felt like for her. Did she feel trapped in the checkout lane, stuck between the cart and her gum-stealing daughter? Did my audacity in taking items without permission, grabbing what I wanted, frighten her? Or did concern about gossip—that some neighbor had seen—overwhelm any thought I might be innocent, at least innocent of intentionally stealing anything? Probably not that—her social standing in the neighborhood didn't mean much to her. My mother chatted with neighbors across our fence, but she didn't go out with girlfriends much or join committees. She stayed in the house and talked on the phone with relatives while ironing or folding laundry.

Feeling trapped caused her fury, I think. A fear of needing to apologize to a manager about her unruly child, our calm routine for the day completely disrupted. Once all that panic was discharged in the parking lot, maybe she felt relief—now she could go home, make her calls, take her pill, and then nap, all with a good excuse.

***

The grocery store changed for me after that: I didn't ride the front of the cart as much and I got hit less. But I did continue to pilfer gum. I snuck it into my pocket while the checkout lady searched for prices and my mother looked through her purse for coupons. I suppose I wanted to be noticed, to be caught for something real and receive a fair punishment. Possibly I just wanted the soft pink gum, to be with Bazooka Joe and his friends, and to know my fortune. I savored the risk and even planned to cry and plead "I forgot!" when found out. Weeks went past though, and neither Mom nor the cashier caught me—or, at least, no one cared to comment.

Just a Hum in the Background

At night my mother and I crawled into her bed with potato chips and a bowl of her homemade dip between us. The family dog hopeful at our feet, tail thumping. We ignored his begging and concentrated on our reading material: me with my Little House books, Mom with her *Good Housekeeping* and *McCall's*.

A radio taking up most of the nightstand played next to her—the host's voice soothing and indistinct, just a hum in the background. My mother listened closely though, and looked up from her magazine if callers with familiar problems got through to her favorite call-in show. The women upset about their hearts racing every time they left the house or their husbands not listening to them were her favorites. She'd lift her hand in a *be quiet* signal if I crinkled the potato chip bag too loudly, her head turned towards the wood console of the radio as if listening to a friend.

Every now and then my father peeked in with a comment. "It's a damn library in here," he'd say, or "When's she going to bed?" Then he'd shake his head and return to the basement and his TV. Back to the shows he watched from an easy chair, a bottle of Pabst clutched tight against his body. Sometimes we'd find him asleep like that: chin drooping to his chest, rising and falling with each breath as if in a continuous nod, some constant agreement with the room, the bottle of beer tilting, tilting, but never spilling.

He was wrong about it being a library in there. We had that radio after all—the confident male questions and hesitant feminine answers giving the evening a certain cadence. And there was our creamy onion dip and the bag of salty chips on the blanket between us as we read. One chip after another dipped into the dish, our hands occasionally colliding when we reached in at the same time. The thunk of my mother's wedding ring against the side of the metal bowl a harsh sound in the quiet bedroom.

Seeking Our Fortunes

It's the sounds of solitaire that are most hypnotic: the ruffle of cards against each other as they're dealt, the slow tap of a fingernail against the deck in contemplation, the harmony of shuffling for a new game. Or maybe it's the patterns: the red-then-black or black-then-red of the king, queen, jack; the slow buildup of diamonds and spades; the repetition of the constant counting to three. It's easy to imagine those first games in the mid-1700s as a kind of fortune telling, the spread of cards across the table reminiscent of a tarot reading, and the study of each play a divination. Easy to envision how a lonesome player might find meaning in the cards. *Ah, the queen! Now, that's lucky. Notice how often she comes up. And look at all those hearts; surely my desires will soon come true!*

***

Sister Marion McGillicudy leaned back in her desk chair, her holy habit draped heavy on her body like a weight to be borne, her hands folded away inside the enormous sleeves. She presented a study in contrasts; the black and white of her dress emphasized her pale skin, and her large forehead stood out against the thin strip of dark hair nearly overshadowed by her white coif and black veil. Her behavior towards me had always matched the sharp variance of her garb. Some days she skewed kind, her apple cheeks puffed out in a smile as she greeted me or explained a lesson, while other days—most days, really—she was harsh, her features firm as she chastised me throughout the day for talking out of turn, for my penmanship, or for a dozen other imperfections.

The night of my seventh-grade parent-teacher conference in 1973, my mother sat beside me and across from Sister Marion. She let Sister know my father had left and that they'd soon be divorcing. My mother clutched her purse to her stomach, her shoulders hunched against the shame of her news. This was Sister Marion's predictive moment. Her tidy desk between us, Sister Marion settled her face into a benevolent countenance, looked my mother over, and said, "I knew something was wrong with her."

I was the only kid in the class with divorcing parents and hadn't told anyone. Since Sister Marion had sent home several notes complaining of rule infractions (wrinkled blouses, papers turned in late) and problems on the playground (chasing boys), my mother felt she should know. Mom trusted the clergy of St. Gregory the Great. She'd even met with our priest the day my father left her a note saying he couldn't take it anymore and was leaving. No explanation of *it* was included, although I, sick with secret knowledge, believed it pertained to a woman I'd seen him kiss at a party, and the low sweet way he talked on the phone whenever Mom left the house. Father Paul had counseled my mother to go home, focus on her housework and prayer, and wait for my father to do the right thing—to come back. While my mother looked to the priest for help, I played games of solitaire betting my father's return against my wins. In these early, changeable days I conjured a happy, carefree life for my mother and me, living our lives without my father's controlling anger. She wouldn't even need her pills anymore, I predicted, since there'd no longer be a reason to cry or get nervous.

***

I didn't think my behavior was the problem at school; I thought Sister Marion was out to get me. There was the grammar test I'd messed up—she'd written cruel comments on it. Even now, I don't remember what, only the injustice of her words, and how she insisted I have it signed by a parent. I tore it up instead. At home I told my mother what happened and showed her the ripped pieces. Uncharacteristically, she wrote a note claiming the test had been misplaced. Sister Marion looked from Mom's writing to me several times the morning I handed her the note before she folded and placed it in her desk drawer. Distrust—magnified eyes locked on me, brows raised high, and lips set tight—written on her face, she nodded me to my seat without speaking.

Our relationship worsened the afternoon I became so engrossed in a book that I didn't hear the call to take out math papers. Sister Marion, assuming intentional disobedience, came over to my desk and completed what she referred to as "an elephant sweep," stretching her arms out long, putting her hands together, and shoving everything off my desk. The loud crashing and tumbling of the day's accumulation of texts and folders and pencils onto the classroom floor startled me out of my trance. I jumped up, quickly sat back down, and then, hands shaking and heart thundering in my chest and head, I stared at the floor, afraid to look up at the furious teacher who stood over me. Around me I heard the low giggles of the boys and the loud shaming silence of the girls.

I wonder what Sister Marion felt as she sent my books cascading into the aisle. Her heart must have been racing from the exertion of her tantrum. Did she relish the power as she stood above me? Hands on her hips and chest heaving, she shouted, "Pick everything up, now!" Did she feel pleased when she turned, habit spinning wide around her, and marched to the front of the room again? She was queen of this game, holding every card, certain her instructions would be followed. The classroom became quiet except for the sounds of me picking up books and folders, hunting for pencils, moving around the desk, searching for my things. The other children's feet and legs pointed dutifully toward Sister Marion. Their hands, I knew, were instinctively folded on their desks—just as I was sure all eyes and ears strained toward me, the unspoken question so loud I could almost taste its salty harshness.

Will she cry?

My expression, I hoped, revealed no emotion, and I bit the inside of my cheek to keep it that way. The kids called me "Stone" for this habit of keeping my face impassive; I hated the nickname but refused to shed tears for the delight of Sister Marion or my classmates. I would not. Sister Marion began her math instruction calmly, only the redness where her cheeks and forehead met her wimple suggesting anything other than her usual icy composure.

During quiet reading time the next week, Sister Marion, strolling up and down the aisles, noticed I was reading Betty Smith's *A Tree Grows in Brooklyn*, a book I'd checked out from our school's library. Without a word she pulled it from my hands and began ripping the paperback apart in front of the paralyzed class, a frightening yet comical performance with pages falling to the ground and Sister straining over the waxy cover. When she finally grew tired and the area around her feet and the nearby desktops became littered with Smith's paragraphs and chapters (the jacket still intact in her hand), she dragged me by the arm to the principal's office. I imagine there must have been sound in this scene. Sister must have shouted questions, students must have made exclamations of surprise, and I must have said something, made some defense of my choice in reading. However, try as I might, I only have a visual of her angry hands throttling the book, the pages of type splayed open to face the class, and sister tearing them off, one after another—wanting so badly to destroy the thing.

It didn't go well for Sister Marion in the principal's office. The librarian, Sister Barbara, joined our group just as Father Paul instructed me to sit down and offered Sister some tea. Sister Barbara's upset about the ruined book was clear the second she saw its remains on Father Paul's desk. I was an avid reader and spent most recesses in the library instead of out on the playground. Sister Barbara had recommended the book to me. Her cheeks blushed and I caught a glare thrown towards Sister Marion before she turned her attention to Father Paul and asked, "What on earth happened to one of my perfectly good books?"

Father Paul, by way of answering, looked at me and said, "You make your way back to class now."

Later, I learned Sister Marion viewed the book as scandalous. It took me several close readings throughout the next year to understand that she meant the scene in which the heroine, Francie Nolan, is attacked in a stairwell by the pervert the neighborhood fears. Francie's mother rescues her and shoots the pedophile, but not before the man's exposed penis touches Francie's leg. The horror of the touch mediated when Francie's father swabs the spot with carbolic acid. Now, though, I wonder if there was more—if the real issue involved the low-class, Irish Nolans themselves. If the father's alcoholism, the family's poverty, and the ragged children were what Sister Marion found most shameful.

***

At the parent-teacher conference, Mom tried to help me out. I had an assigned seat in the back row of the classroom, the solitary girl amongst a group of troublemaking boys, and often complained about how I couldn't concentrate. Mom asked Sister to change my seat to encourage better focus. Sister Marion sighed, glancing at me. Her kind smile pasted on, she said, "Everyone has to take their turn in the back."

Why didn't I jump up and shout *It's not fair?* Or, *Why doesn't Katie with perfect handwriting and two parents ever have to sit there?* Why didn't my mom stand up and insist? At the time, though, children and parents rarely questioned or argued with teachers, and they never contradicted nuns. I stayed silent, traced the markings on the desk with my fingers, and did not let either woman see my face. Sister Marion's cruelties seemed all too similar to those of the neighborhood kids who'd begun chanting the title of the movie *Divorce His, Divorce Hers* once news leaked of my parents' split. And my mother was likely to amplify any upset I expressed with her own woes and a night of drinking. Mostly though, I found emotions both dangerous and ineffective: signs of anger (crinkled eyes, sucked in lips) led to punishment and tears led to teasing. Better to keep my head down, withdraw inside, and embrace being "Stone."

***

At home, with my mother working during the day and going out to bars at night, I played solitaire for hours, the time ticking by, the dog nestled at my leg, the safe rhythms of the cards, the counting, and the repetition blocking out my worries and distracting me from the low, creaking noises of the settling house.

My grandmothers liked to play solitaire. Mom's mom, Grandma Nowicki, played a version called Kings' Corners. The idea of getting all of the cards out was the same, but the layout was in a square instead of a straight line. Grandma played at her kitchen table late into the night after Grandpa went to bed. The brightly focused glow from a desk lamp shining slant and making a circle of light for the hand she dealt. Her tan, plastic tablecloth had a pattern pressed into it, and the print from newspapers rubbed off in the small recessed squares. On overnights, when I sat watching her play, I'd use my fingernails to rub off bits of the black ink, and, more than likely, dirt, making designs or writing my name. The temptation to write swearwords was always strong. I resisted though, waiting for the velvet or plush naps of couches and chairs on which to write *shithead* over and over—the expletive my mother used when referencing my father—or *damn* or *hell*, the cusswords my friends and I more regularly experimented with. Words I could erase with the brush of my hand.

My dad's mother, Grandma Dora, had a cup of tea with a graham cracker and played solitaire before bed every night that I slept over. She counted three cards from the top of the deck, hit them on the table for luck, and then considered what to do. The top card had to be played first, and she never glanced at the other cards she held. "Why know if nothing can be done?" she'd ask when I begged her to peek. But I wanted to look, especially if it seemed like she'd lose. I wanted to see which play might have changed everything. If she couldn't sleep, I'd hear her bring the deck out again, the sounds floating down the long hallway of her and Grandpa's trailer to the back room where I slept. Grandpa's rhythmic, predictable snores punctuated the snap of cards while I drifted to sleep.

In earlier years, well before seventh grade, Mom

and I played double solitaire in the evening, the two-deck game similar to playing alone, except that the aces in the middle were shared. My father, still living with us, drank beer and watched TV in the basement. If it got late, he dozed in his chair, the bottle still clutched in his hand—leaning, leaning, leaning, but not quite falling. In Mom's room, low music from her radio wove through our absorption as we dealt cards on the wrinkles of the blankets, the patterns upset if either of us stretched or moved a leg across the covers. A few times we played out. Just eight piles centered between us, arranged by suit and ace to king, our excitement bigger than the memory of who finished first.

***

After my father left for good, my mother focused on her grief. Games of chance and the supposed comfort of the church faded away. I want to recapture those days, that post-separation season when my mother's drinking—which had simply been a wifely accompaniment to my dad's—became something else. There is the echo of my mother's key struggling in the back door's flimsy lock of our house on 54th Street in Milwaukee. The house stood second from the corner, white with red shutters. The small kitchen had diamond-patterned vinyl flooring and a Formica table with metal edging. I burned the floor with a lit match once, although I denied it. My brothers were away at college—leaving the upstairs bedrooms empty and the rest of the house quiet.

Blame for my father's departure had fallen on The Other Woman, but now I wonder about the note he'd left saying he couldn't take it anymore, about the myriad definitions of the word *it*. I wish there'd been another paragraph of explanation. Looking back, I can see the odd gift of all that blame though. Blame, with its attendant hurt and anger, is so much better than digging to the shifting, murky bottom of *it*.

After my father left, my mother began to frequent taverns, and I spent evenings listening for her steps on the porch, waiting for the clink of metal against wood before her key entered the lock. She'd jangle and fumble the keys as she twisted the doorknob right then left. If her struggle in the dark went on too long, I'd open the door. Holding her purse tight against her body with one hand and gripping the useless key in the other, she'd say, "Oh, Joanne," when I appeared, as if she expected or hoped for someone else. Someone else awake after midnight and waiting for her inside the empty house. Someone else watching the clock and playing games with time—she'll be home before the minute hand reaches the twelve, before I finish a chapter, before I can say ten Hail Marys.

My mother was not a sleepy or funny drunk; her personality changed and she became repetitive, quick to anger and impossible to reason with. When upset, she'd phone family and friends for support, no matter the hour. If the cause was my fault, she tossed my toys in the garbage or insisted I couldn't go to school the next day.

At first, I didn't associate the word *drunk* with her. Even with all of the after-bar clumsiness and flu-like mornings, I didn't get it. Then one night, listening to her on the other side of the door calling to her keys, "Come on now, where are you?" it hit me. Standing in our alcove, I stared at our shoes lined up on the rubber mat and at our jackets hanging from the hooks on the wall above. Shoes and jackets ready for the next day, for the safe routine of work and school. Adults might drink too much and act silly, drive too fast, or argue with their wives, but being a drunk seemed darker, and so much worse.

***

Eventually my mother began working at a factory and I found other ways to keep busy. I befriended two girls, Nan and Amanda, and we became proficient at skipping school. The three of us crept to the edge of our school's property while the boys played football and the other girls jumped rope, and then we slipped behind a row of bushes and climbed over a fence to reach the neighborhood beyond. At Amanda's, her mother also away at work, we stole cigarettes and made peanut butter sandwiches. We returned before the end of lunch recess, fading into the lines of kids waiting for the bell, our secrets left us satisfied and confident for the rest of the afternoon. Finally done with pleasing her, I found Sister Marion much less menacing.

Our leaving wasn't necessarily a secret from everyone. Two Christmases ago, my dad shared a story with me. We were in his living room. There was a fake tree sparkling with lights decorated with baubles and the tatted snowflakes my grandmother made. The room buzzed with the conversations of siblings and stepsiblings, nieces, nephews, grandchildren and great grandchildren. He told me how, after he left my mother—left us—he'd watch me at recess. I attended a private school and his employer had assigned him a pipe-covering job at a small public school on the same grounds. He described the green jacket I wore.

I wish I'd asked my dad if he watched us disappear behind those bushes and, if he did, what he told himself about our journey; if he found excuses to remain where he could watch for our return, even saying his own prayers for safety. I wonder what fortune he predicted for me.

***

Was there something wrong with me, as Sister Marion had suggested? I suppose, but it was more than just the absence of my father. I didn't fit at the Catholic school for a whole host of reasons. My short, fine hair stuck to my head in a time of long, fluffy curls and waves; my sloppy cursive made As that didn't close and wide, uneven loops of Ts and Ls; and my socks fell to my ankles instead of staying up nice and snug below my knees the way Katie's and even Nan's and Amanda's always did.

There was something wrong with how I put my mother to bed at night when she drank too much and the way I lied for her—to my grandmothers about where she went at night and to her work when I called in sick for her. And something wrong with how many nights I asked Nan if I could stay at her house, anything to avoid another night in my own home. Maybe I deserved the spot in the back with those naughty boys who threw spitballs and made faces when Sister wrote on the board. They made me giggle, and Sister's godly ears straightaway turned to me, singling me out for punishment. As if I'd laughed with no provocation, just a titter to announce a glorious day, to bother those angelic boys arranged around me.

There was certainly something wrong with Sister Marion. I still picture her in her dark habit and full wimple at a time when other nuns were starting to wear street clothes or at least a dress with a simple veil. What reading of scripture nourished such rectitude and obvious disgust with my badly combed hair, my ill-fitting uniform, and me in general? How was I not someone she could care for, not someone she thought worthy?

I'm curious to know what happened that day in Father Paul's office after he sent me back to class and Sister Marion had to face his judgment, the librarian's anger, and that wrecked book. Curious about what embarrassment she suffered in the convent that evening—or if she saw herself as justified, as saving impressionable girls from literature that would lead to impure thoughts. She didn't return the next year, nor did any of the nuns, as their order broke with the priests of our school. Our paths diverged, but in retrospect, there may have been another way to interpret her comment at the seventh-grade conference. Perhaps her declaration of, "I knew something was wrong with her" was gentler than memory colors it. Either way, the inclusion of the words, *with her*, makes the phrase personal, much like a card flipping over and telling a fortune.

Love Lost

Timmy and I were high school seniors when we dated. He went to St. Thomas More, the Catholic boys' school, just a few miles from St. Mary's Academy, the girls' school I attended. Since St. Mary's started earlier, the boys from TM dropped off their girlfriends or sisters and then stayed to flirt until the bell rang and we girls crossed under the gates inscribed with "Knowledge and Virtue United" and into our school day. There was plenty of mingling.

We went to homecoming—at his school, of course—his cousin drove as Timmy didn't have his license yet. I remember sitting on Timmy's lap in the brightly lit social hall, gray and blue bunting floating from the ceiling, glasses of soda scattered on the tables, friends surrounding us. When I lean away from Timmy to whisper with a friend, I can feel his arms tight around my waist.

Timmy, as best I recall, was a true love, but he certainly wasn't the first boy I ever kissed. My first real kiss—a French kiss—happened after a different Thomas More gathering, the first dance of freshman year, 1976.

***

The band had finished for the night. I'd been dancing with a boy I'd only just met. He walked me down the hall, past the lockers and tables piled with coats, until we stood on the school steps—anonymous in the dark, boys and girls streaming past us. I turned to say goodbye before running to meet my ride. He bobbed toward me. I realized he wanted more than a friendly hug, that what I'd dreamt of and read about in *Cosmopolitan* was about to happen.

His face came toward me—his mouth wide open, his teeth clanked against mine, and we kissed. French kissed. I'd fantasized about this kiss for years, although usually picturing it as a more delicate experience. In truth, I found the whole confusion of lips and teeth and tongues disconcerting. I worried about my nose and what to do with my neck, which hurt, as I hadn't arranged the angle correctly and didn't want to interrupt my new friend to rearrange. Anyway, all too soon, I had to break our embrace and run down the school steps to my best friend's sister impatiently beeping her car's horn.

***

I no longer recall the boy's name, or even his facial features above his nose. Only his open mouth, those straight, bright teeth, and that tongue—which may have been somewhat larger and heavier than average—remain.

I doubt we talked or dated after that night. I remember the drive home, the teasing from my friend and her sister. I didn't mind, wrapped in my cloak of sensual pleasure—unsure the kiss was categorically enjoyable, but definitely wanting it to happen again. I felt I'd left some middle-school shadow behind, passed an important milestone, and could stand outside the school gates in the morning a little wiser. Secret knowledge in my eyes as I watched boys drive up to flirt with the older girls before first bell.

***

Timmy from senior year had messy blond hair and an overbite. He was tall and the sleeves of his blazers landed right above his wrist bones in a very sweet way. We mostly fooled around in front of his mother's Milwaukee bungalow in my mother's Chevy Impala after I drove him home from our Young Christian Life meetings. I'd glide to the curb, put the car in park, and we'd make out. The porch light above his family's front door a welcoming beacon that shadowed our faces, until it began to flicker on and off, on and off, more and more rapidly the longer we tried to ignore it.

I imagined Timmy's mom's worries floating through her living room window, past the azaleas asleep in the front yard, and into my car with its undependable heater, tinny AM radio, and sporadically revving engine. Her presence, like Jesus—the unseen guest at every meal—hovered between us as we whispered and kissed.

One sad night when Timmy embraced me, his right hand stayed on the armrest. I could see it there, the arm bent with tension, pulling him away from me and towards the house, and I knew what was coming. I knew even before he said, eyes lowered, that he had to get in early for homework. My drive home that evening through the south side streets was long. I tried to convince myself I'd misjudged the situation; but of course I hadn't. Timmy broke up with me before school the next morning, and our paths didn't cross again. I don't know that I ever told my mother about our breakup—my adolescent revenge for her continued drinking was to share nothing about my life with her—but I pictured Timmy's mom's happiness when he began coming home at a decent time. The porch light once again became a friendly greeting to all who walked past in the dark.

I think about Timmy sometimes. I'm both disappointed and relieved to find out he's not traceable through Facebook or Google. Timmy is the last boy I dated before turning eighteen and graduating from high school. He closed the chapter that began with my first dance and first kiss. After graduation I worked in a factory for the summer—day after day of hungover box making—and then left for college. There were no more porch lights and no more voices calling us in for the night—still, we never quite left those first neighborhoods.

I'm left wondering if anyone ever looks for me. Maybe even that forgotten boy on the steps of Thomas More. The boy left waiting for his parents' car to pull alongside the curb, one more in an endless stream of vehicles picking up kids from the dance and taking them home again.

The Silences We Keep

During my freshman year in high school, before my mother remarried and we moved away, my dad occasionally parked down the block from the house on 54th Street, waiting in his shiny red car to drive me to school. I remember feeling a stomach-achy rush of fear when I spotted his car. Not because of anything untoward in his relationship with me, but because of how my mother would handle knowledge of our seeing each other. Her hurt at his betrayal was endless, and I became her living, breathing, always present representative of injury. I suppose Dad and I commented on the weather or the long wait between buses while we journeyed down Oklahoma Avenue all the way to St. Mary's Academy. My clearest memories are of the sound of the door as I pulled it closed, smooth vinyl seats in a car that had never been part of our family with keys that had never hung from the hook above the coat rack, and his pleasant "Hey, Kid" as I settled in before he returned his gaze to the road. Neither of us ever remarked on his surprise appearance or the change in his living arrangements.

I recognize my own complicity, the way I also turned my eyes to the street winding out of our neighborhood instead of initiating any meaningful conversation. I knew how to hold my tongue. On the day he'd filled his car with boxes and moved out, he asked me if I'd miss him and I didn't say a word in reply, protecting him from my answer.

Now, I wonder what it cost him to park down the block and wait for me. He couldn't have been sure I'd even appear—in those days, I babysat for cousins that lived nearby and often slept at their house. He also risked my mother driving past him on her own way to work, recognizing him and causing some sort of scene. I wonder about his own hours—if memory serves, he started early. Did he make some excuse, arrive late just to drive me to school? It seems unlikely there was any such thing as flexible hours in his trade as a pipe coverer. And yet, there he was. I'm curious about the scene in his own kitchen. His new wife packing his lunch box. Her awareness that he was leaving to see his daughter. Did she give her blessing or did tension rise between them?

It is only with the passage of years that I can view his arrival to pick me up through any wider lens than that of my own discomfort. When I look through the eyes of a working parent and imagine the extra time necessary to pick up a sullen, anxious teenager, I recognize how difficult not only coming to our house must have been, but also how complicated the entire process of leaving us was—and that I fit into those complications. He made efforts, in his own confused, quiet way, to see me. Twice, maybe three times, I'd even looked out the long, thin windows of my school's gymnasium to see him watching me play volleyball for my school's team. He never came in. And I didn't go out to greet him. I'd never considered our relationship extended two ways.

A memory came back to me recently involving my dad. We're at Lyon's Park on 55th Street, just two blocks from our house. I'm at the playground with him. Maybe my mother has asked him to take me somewhere. Maybe she just wants to clean the house once and for all without interruptions. Maybe grandparents are coming over later and she needs to get something done. Or maybe my grandfather and older brothers accompanied us but reside just outside of memory. I retain only this: the sweep of the swing growing higher and higher as my father pushed me, until he under-ducked and arrived at the other side to face me and laugh. And me, pumping my legs towards him again and again.

How Pretty
She Looked

My mother had great legs. And oh, could she dance! On summer Sundays, the year between my mother's divorce and second marriage, she and my aunt took me to church festivals. They claimed they went for the outdoor masses, the chicken dinners, and the music, but the real goal—even prayer—was to meet a new man. Someone brave enough to leave the bar at the back of the dance tent, walk over, and introduce himself to two women and one small girl reading a book. Mostly, though, the men kept to themselves, and the dance floor filled with women holding each other. My mother and Aunt Delores were always the best dancers. Pantyhose emphasized the long lines of their legs and red lipstick stood out bright against their smiles. Decked out in pretty dresses that flared when they turned, they polkaed and waltzed around the tent, doing intricate footwork to impress each other and the watching men.

My grandmother, when brought along for the afternoon, sat at a folding table clutching her purse, the same plastic cup of warm beer in front of her for the entire afternoon. Sometimes Aunt Delores begged her to dance. Grandma reluctantly gave her purse to me, cautioning me not to let it out of my sight before she'd go along to the parking-lot dance floor. I watched her laugh, the music swaying around her, as they two-stepped throughout the makeshift hall. When Grandma returned she settled herself into the chair, took back her purse, and sipped her flat beer. She'd accuse Delores of stepping on her feet, or tell me to sit up straight, or my mother not to laugh so loud.

"Barbara," she'd shush, shifting in the hard chair, "that's a barroom laugh." My mother would look away, pretend not to hear, and take a long swallow of the Pabst in her plastic cup.

I wanted the dancing to go on forever, the women twirling the afternoon away while I read and Gram clutched her purse. What I feared was the trip home. The Sundays Mom dropped off Grandma and Delores and then said she had to make a stop.

"Where?" I would ask, stomach shrinking up tight long before she answered.

"I just want to stop a minute."

She stared straight ahead as she drove, lost in her own thoughts. The dancing, the swirl of her pretty skirts, and the smiles of the men who'd noticed, probably left her wanting more than another night alone with her kid, nothing to do but watch TV until she fell asleep. Maybe her mother's biting words fueled her desire to be anywhere but home.

I sat forgotten in the passenger seat. Any more questions, experience told me, any claims of homework or a tummy ache made her stubborn—a ticket to an even worse evening.

We always drove to a tavern, either Veteran's Park or The Blue Canary, and then—swearing to be right back—she left and I sat alone in the car, unable to concentrate on my book, counting the cars as they drove past. Promising myself she'd be out before ten blue cars passed me, or maybe fifteen, or for sure by time I said thirty Hail Mary's and an Our Father. I kept my head low, afraid of being noticed as the day faded to dusk and then evening. When I ran out of prayers I fantasized about what my grandmother might say if she could see me. If only I was brave enough to tell her.

***

How the daylight filtered through the big tent seams as my mother spun across the dance floor was on my mind when, years later, I drove to St. Luke's Hospital in Milwaukee to see my mother after she'd fallen and injured herself. Actually, it was the third day after her accident before I made the drive from my home in Hartland, an hour west of the hospital.

My mother had fallen in a neighbor's driveway— her boyfriend, Ray, had told me over the phone. She'd broken her neck. "But not one of those bad broken necks," he reported. No, he didn't know if she'd been drinking or not. Ray mentioned he was the only one listed on the hospital's emergency form and that the staff were unaware she had three children.

I understood this omission; we'd not had an easy relationship since those church festival days. After my mother remarried, she'd continued to drink heavily and take copious amounts of prescription medication for depression, anxiety, and sleep issues. A medical scare involving esophageal bleeding had initiated twenty years of sobriety which ended following my stepfather's death. Through it all, she continued to abuse her prescriptions. She was skilled at using different forms of her name with different doctors as well as manipulating mail-order drug services. Now in her eighties, she lived on her own and dated Ray.

Since I lived the closest, and because I was the girl—daughters take care of their mothers, my grandmother preached—I was the one who checked on her the most. Bill, my eldest brother, and his wife lived two hours away. He called her infrequently and visited a couple times a year. Steven, our middle brother, was close with Mom and talked with her at least daily. But he lived alone in a cabin in the northern part of the state and would be too drunk at any given time to help in an emergency. Even my mother would have realized this.

I, on the other hand, stopped over weekly. I kept my coat on, made meaningless small talk, and shared nothing of my life—all while my eyes darted around the room, scanning for beer cans or other signs of trouble. We were both keen for my lunch hour to end so I could leave and return to work. I suppose she dreaded me catching her still in pajamas, her face baggy with sleep, the sink full of dishes, and wondered what I'd find to criticize this time. I became one more in a lengthy line of people telling her what to do with her life and how she should live it; all of us suggesting change after change she could make instead of just letting her be. Now, looking back,

I see that this is what made her close to my alcoholic brother—with Steven she could be herself. He wouldn't expect or ask for anything different.

With me she needed to be on guard. I repeatedly questioned her choice to live alone, and even had someone from Milwaukee County's Department on Aging stop over. I viewed myself as helpful, but from her point of view—well, it seemed I'd become the wicked stepmother to my own mother, always causing a problem with my interfering ways. While it's true I kept my coat on during visits, it's also true that she didn't invite me to sit down.

I wasn't surprised my name didn't appear on that form. In fact, I was somewhat relieved.

"I'm sorry you had to handle this," I told Ray the day he called with the news. But really, I wanted nothing to do with the hospital. This was not my mother's first admission in the past year. Once, Ray took my mother to the emergency room because her legs hurt and she kept falling. She was admitted and diagnosed with malnutrition. Next there was a two-week stay when a dog bite became septic and turned into an antibiotic-resistant staph infection. Only a few months before this current crisis, when snow still covered her yard, there was yet another admission for confusion and a urinary tract infection. During every hospital stay, I'd tell nurses her history of addictions and talk with social workers about options available for follow-up care. Each time the staff, along with Bill and I, recommended a move to assisted living or even a group home. By the end of every stay, however, she'd rally and pass all mental status assessments.

Free to make her own decisions, my mother would return home.

***

I took the dog for a walk instead of calling St. Luke's after Ray gave me the news about my mother's "not bad" broken neck. It was my favorite time of day, the light changing throughout the neighborhood as the sun rose, the houses sleepy looking with their curtains still drawn, all the yards quiet. After we returned—my own daughters still asleep and my husband already at work—I got the dog fresh water and continued to delay. Made my coffee, ate breakfast, and started some wash. I realized, as I completed each action, this might not be how I'd want to tell this story—a story I'd want to rewrite to say I jumped up and drove to the hospital. That isn't what I did though. Instead, I poured more coffee and folded clothes. All these stall tactics so I wouldn't have to contact the hospital, explain who I was, gather the information, update my brother, and disrupt my life yet again.

***

When I eventually called, a nurse informed me my mother was now on the neurology floor, standard procedure with neck injuries. She questioned my relationship to the patient, and I suggested she look back in the chart to the nursing and social services notes. I knew she'd see records of conversations with me dating from other stays and feel more comfortable talking.

My mother had bumps, bruises, and a fractured

neck, the nurse eventually told me. Surgery didn't seem necessary—a neck brace would be enough, so long as she kept it on and took care of herself. Her blood alcohol concentration was elevated, and as of morning rounds she didn't know her location, our current president, or the day of the week. The nurse asked if my mother regularly drank. I confirmed this and suggested they run a medication screen to see what else remained in her system. Again I referenced the history in the red flip chart I hoped she perused as we talked. In the past, drug screens had found barbiturates as well as elevated levels of sleeping, antidepressant, and antianxiety medications in her system. The results often didn't match her current prescriptions. The nurse doubted my mother could live alone anymore and suggested I talk with the social worker.

It all felt horribly familiar.

When I got off the phone, I called my husband and brother to tell them what had happened. I decided not to visit the hospital. Both men agreed, my brother adding: "She'll still be drunk. There's no point."

***

The next morning a new nurse told me my mother had slept poorly and walked the halls during the night looking for beer. Due to safety concerns, they planned to have a sitter in the room at all times, beginning that afternoon. After she explained the role of a sitter, she asked me the same questions as yesterday's nurse.

In the afternoon I drove to the hospital. All those memories of my mother dancing kept me company while I maneuvered through summer construction on the expressway and again on the city streets. St. Luke's was a large complex—bigger than the town I lived in, it seemed. The brick and glass buildings were forever going through renovations and, to me, confusing additions. Once parked in the hospital's multi-level garage, I walked down the long corridors, following the green tiles leading to neurology until I arrived at the right elevator. I'd never been to neurology. My mother's other stays were down the blue tiles of general admission. Without the colored tiles to lead me, I didn't think I'd ever find my way back out of the hospital.

The drapes were pulled in Mom's room. There were no cards or flowers, nothing personal to mark the place as hers. A whiteboard hung on a wall listing the date and the name of the doctor, current nurse, aide, and sitter. Smiley faces squared off a section that indicated *general diet* and *no allergies*. The TV played without sound; the serious faces of soap opera characters were childhood familiar and a comfort as I put down my purse and settled myself into the room. A young woman I assumed to be the sitter sat in a chair close to the bed doing a crossword. She looked up, said, "Hi," and resumed the puzzle. My mother had required sitters before, and this was what they did: read magazines, played games, and pretended to be invisible until needed.

My mother's eyes were closed and she appeared to be asleep. Both were discolored, one ringed by blotches of emerging purples and blues, the other with waves of greenish-black, blue, and yellow extending from her nose towards the outer edge of her eye. She had a cervical collar on and it pushed up her head, making her usually long face look fat and full-moon shaped. She wore a hospital gown and gray hospital socks with non-skid bottoms. The sheet and blanket covered her middle, but her feet and thin legs, lined with deep-purple varicose veins, stuck out.

The varicose veins unnerved me. Nothing about them was recognizable from the days my aunt and mother danced their energetic polkas and gentle waltzes. I allowed the legs to distract me, to keep me from focusing on the swollen face and the inflexible, cloth-covered neck brace that pushed her chin up, creating a doubled effect where none had existed before. The brace and the fracture it represented symbolized the deal changer here—if the nurse was correct, making this stay different from the rest.

***

My mother's body looked slender under the sheet. She'd always had a decent shape, but her hair had changed in the last few years. Our activities had once revolved around weekly visits to the beauty shop—owned by Aunt Delores—to have her hair set and combed out. The same soap operas played while the women got their hair done each Friday. The volume turned up, the antics of the characters part of the ongoing dialogue in the room. Now Mom's hair hung limp and dirty. The change in her legs, however, with their maps of veins, was even more striking. I had often coveted her slim legs, had wished I had them instead of my own bulky ones. I flashed on a time in my late teens: we were at somebody's picnic and a softball game had started. My mother, whom I had never seen participate in anything, got up to play. I was afraid, waiting for something to go wrong—a fall while running or a ball to the head—but everything went well. She batted and ran the bases, just like anyone else. She looked good with her shapely legs and white shorts, running with her tongue sticking out a bit, and her right shoulder leaning forward, the same way mine does. Looking just like everyone else's mom.

I wondered if she'd noticed the veins now criss-crossing her legs and, foolishly, if the change corre-lated to her hair becoming so dull, so lifeless.

"Mom?"

She didn't respond.

"Do you mind if I get a soda?" the sitter asked. "I'll be right back."

I nodded and quashed my desire to tell the girl, "She didn't used to look this way."

***

When the sitter came back with her drink I left to find the unit's social worker. The staff paged her and we met in her office. While pulling out a chair for me, she updated me on Mom's status. "She can be discharged as soon as all the tests are back," she said. "But we'd like her to have a psychiatric consult first."

The doctor believed my mother should have already detoxed from the alcohol and any medications in her system and speculated about dementia. I agreed to the consultation, but doubted it would be accurate. This place was too big and too busy for anyone to remember other admissions. During past stays, Mom took days to orient to her surroundings. When she came in on her own—the stay for leg pain—she snuck in her own medication for anxiety and sleep. She got away with it until the staff saw Ray getting pills from her purse. The social worker assured me we'd talk again and added, "Anyway, we can't discharge until the sitter is safely gone for at least twenty-four hours."

After our conversation, I returned to my mother's room. The sitter continued her work on the cross-word puzzle and a tray of untouched food rested on the swing table next to the bed. Mom's eyes remained closed, but she had turned over and now gently snored. She didn't respond when I pulled up the sheet and blanket, shaking them to get the wrin-kles out, and letting the covers settle down around her, or when I rested my hand on her shoulder before leaving.

Being gentle seemed easier with her in this safe place where I needn't worry about her drinking or driving. Much easier to touch her and whisper some-thing as tender as *goodbye* when I wasn't afraid this might be the day I'd get the telephone call telling me she'd harmed someone.

I stopped at her house before going home. The door stood unlocked—so, although it was daytime, I phoned my brother and asked him to stay on the line as I looked around. While we talked, I tossed half cans of food, some spoiled milk, and anything else past expiration from the refrigerator. I noted the stove's burners were missing and described the opened cans of beer in the bedroom, the bottles of pills on the dressers and kitchen table, the stacks of papers and unpaid bills everywhere, and the dog poop on the living room rug. The poop from the dog my mother had never house-trained, the one Ray must have picked up and taken back to his house already.

I sat down on the edge of a chair, heart racing, and told my brother, those glorious two hours away, "It's too much, it's just too much."

The neighbors—Myrna, her grown son, and his two children—spotted me when I took out the garbage. They yelled hello from their driveway, and I walked over to thank them for calling the ambulance. Myrna asked about my mother's injuries and added that they worried about her constantly. Mom had come over to borrow a rake the morning she fell. The grown son and his kids were getting into the car to go shopping and saw the whole thing.

"I guess she might have been drinking," Myrna said. "She didn't seem too steady on her feet. Right, Shawn?" Myrna looked at her son, who nodded, and then continued, "I offered her some breakfast, but all she wanted was that rake. She can be stubborn. Once she got it, she turned to leave and fell straight down." Myrna raised her hand, let it fall, and Shawn took over.

"Straight down, didn't put her hand out at all. The kids thought she died." He shook his head, and they both looked at me.

"Well, we're sure lucky you were here," I said. "I'm sorry your kids saw all that." I felt unsteady myself at this point, the hot embarrassment about my mother's actions as well as concern for Shawn's kids now bubbling up in a way that hadn't occurred to me at the hospital. I wanted to flee, to go home to my family and pretend none of this was happening. Instead, I stayed and told Myrna and Shawn all the ways I'd tried to get my mother help, including contact with her doctors about the medications, Social Services about her house, and even the police about her driving. I didn't say these things because I wanted to chat or unburden myself, but simply so they'd think better of me. So they'd know I had tried to do something. I hoped they'd spread the word to the other neighbors who, I imagined, thought my mother had been abandoned by her children.

***

At home I heard from the hospital. They'd moved my mother to the ICU because her salt levels were too low. This wasn't a crisis, but the salt solution had to be monitored carefully, and an ICU stay was necessary until her numbers improved. Before the nurse hung up she mentioned low salt could cause confusion.

Over the next few days the salt levels improved, but the confusion didn't. My mother flunked the memory portions of the psychological tests and gained a moderate dementia diagnosis. Once they reached this verdict, the hospital wanted her out. Her behavior posed risks, the sitter cost them money, and she couldn't be further fixed. They dismissed the sitter and the social worker found a rehabilitation unit for her neck injury in a nursing home. Not trusting our mother wouldn't demand to go home, my brother and I refused to drive her, thus the staff arranged for a hospital van to transport her. When she refused to get in the van, the social worker requested permission to have her taken in an ambulance against her will.

"Sure, go ahead," I answered.

I stood in my kitchen doing dishes and listening to traffic on the highway beyond the tree line while we spoke. In my mind's eye the hospital nurses huddled next to my mother, trying to coax her into a strange van with a driver she'd never met. I imagined their soft voices as they reminded her she was going to get help with her neck, at a very nice place.

My mother, I knew, would become more obstinate with their every kind word. I felt so very glad not to be there. When the ambulance arrived, the attendants strapped Mom onto a gurney for the ride. This calmed her, the social worker later told me.

***

I didn't meet my mother at the nursing home; didn't go with a suitcase of her clothing, a favorite blanket, or family pictures to help her settle in. I didn't expect her to see my presence there as helpful and feared she'd insist on leaving. My brother, who hadn't visited at all, agreed, but his wife voiced her disgust with the both of us.

"It's what you're supposed to do," she said. If her mother had a broken neck, she'd have been there for the hospital discharge and then met her at the nursing home.

I reminded her we were talking about a woman who denied having children. This made my brother laugh, but my sister-in-law huffed and said, "What will they think when no one is there to greet her?"

When a friend, hearing the saga, asked what my husband did during all this, I was surprised and thought, *Well he worked, of course. What's he got to do with it?* Later, however, I connected my friend's question to my sister-in-law's disgust. Family was supposed to be part of this scene—my brother at the hospital, my spouse nearby for support, all of us helping our mother settle into her new location. But I wanted to take charge and manage all the work with as few complications and voices as possible. I wanted this drama kept separate from my husband and children, from my real life.

***

An administrator called within a few hours, saying my mother refused to settle down, suggesting I come. "Family usually has a calming influence," she told me.

I regretted answering the phone but, my sister-in-law's words still ringing in my ears, said I'd drive over.

The nursing home was in Pewaukee, an upscale community only ten minutes from my home. Several small, pleasant-looking buildings, including my mother's rehab unit, were arranged around court-yards in an attractive setting. A grove of trees grew a short way from the parking lot and wild turkeys were in the yard eating from bird feeders, their long necks reaching for seeds missed by the sparrows and robins. They scattered when I closed the car door. Inside, the nurses' station was at the center of two long hallways ending in sitting areas. My mother walked rapid laps around the chairs and couches, and then up one hallway and down the other. I joined the staff gathered at the nurses' station, all eyes on my mother in her short hospital gown and socks, the neck brace pushing her face up and head forward, her hair still unwashed and uncombed. I introduced myself as "the daughter" to the nurse who seemed in charge. She said, "Your mother won't stop her pacing, and she pushed one of the aides."

"Mom," I called several times when she strode past, but she didn't even turn her head. Finally, I put out my hand, touched her arm, and said, "Mom, it's me, it's Joanne." She stopped and shook my hand away so sharply that I flinched and stepped back, afraid she'd hit me. My mother just looked hard at me, though, stared into my eyes and said, "I know who you are." Then she turned around and I watched her walk back down the long hallway, her destination unclear.

I was peripherally aware of the nurses staring from my mother to me, the bright florescent lights of the hallway, and the tinned pleasant music surrounding us; all I could think about was how much my mother had disliked being seen with bare legs. Again, as when I fretted over her varicose veins in the hospital room, this was an attempt to distract myself. The real issue being the truth of her hurled accusation— so much worse than any slap.

I had worked hard through my adolescence and adulthood to make sure my mother didn't know me— my payback for her neglect and alcoholism. I'd kept my coat on, my face closed, my joys and woes unmentioned.

Despite my polite words to nurses and efforts to look concerned, I was furious about my mother's intrusion into my current life. Furious that it was me, not my brothers, now stuck with this mess—with her. I wanted to be anywhere else but the nursing home hallway, where I stood alone and exposed to the staff huddled together at the nurses' station. Hands in my jacket pockets, I watched my mother retreat. She certainly did know who I was, and I knew she was right to turn and walk away. From a distance, her legs still looked shapely beneath the thin, pink hospital gown.

What We Keep

After my mother's admission to a nursing home, my stepbrother, Marty, said he'd help sort what to keep and what to throw away. So on a late summer day, the leaves just starting to dull with heat and age, we met at the ranch home our parents had shared. Marty's dad, Russ, had built the house for his first family when his children were young—long before he married my mother. Marty brought a cousin and I had my husband, Bruce, along to help with anything heavy.

They arrived just as Bruce and I were lifting the broken garage door. He held it up while I wedged a two-by-four in between the door and the cement floor. The sound of their pick-up's tires on the gravel driveway was a loud interruption to our quiet work. Or it just seemed loud, anxious as I was about spending this day with them. Marty and I barely knew each other, and when we'd spoken on the phone he shared that he hadn't been to the house in years. My mother never liked Russ's kids coming over. Once they'd married, the house became hers she'd believed, and she didn't want the reminder of his previous life. Mom invited my stepsiblings to a meal at Christmas to appease Russ, but often stayed in her room if they dropped by without calling. Even holiday invitations had stopped after his death five years earlier.

Marty organized estate sales for a living, and we poked around the crowded garage while getting used to each other. The cousin told stories about my step-father teaching him and the other boys how to lift weights "right here in this garage." That would have been way before my time.

I'd promised to give Marty items of his father's in exchange for helping us decide what to keep and what to toss into the dumpster in the driveway. Over the last several weeks, my husband and I had moved as much from the house as possible into the breezeway leading into the garage and into the garage itself. Now the area bloated with furniture from both of our families, rows of boxes filled with the record albums my mother collected, multiple sets of dishes purchased from multiple rummage sales, and the usual clutter of rakes, nails, and shovels found in any garage.

A paint-spattered workbench ran the length of the back wall and cupboards covered with pictures from old calendars hung above it, the years rolling by from the late 1950s to the mid-1970s when my mother and I had moved in. The once sunny yellow paint of the cupboards had faded to a dull backdrop for festive shots of families on picnics, men working on cars, and dogs sitting next to fire engines. Signs of the good life greeting our every return.

The discolored tape holding each picture remained strong. Bruce had started ripping down the pictures earlier in the week but had become distracted by another project. Now, towards the side where my stepfather used to park his car, random bits of tape were stuck to the wall with calendar corners attached. We would need to drench the tape in soapy water or scrape it with thin razor blades before we could repaint.

Marty's dad had built the house in the 1950s, when Marty, the eldest of five, was a sophomore in high school. I arrived in the 1970s, years after his parents divorced. I was the youngest of three, a freshman in high school, and the only one left at home to accompany my mother into her second marriage.

I didn't mind the move. My private high school attendance (a long city bus ride away) had already distanced me from neighborhood friends, and enough time had gone by since my dad's departure and brothers' move to college that the house no longer felt raw with memories of birthday parties and holiday celebrations. Besides, my stepfather was a good man—kind to my mother and reserved, yet friendly enough, with me. Even I could see he was a better match for my mom than my dad had been.

I learned to drive the year after we moved in. Russ—perhaps fearing for the safety of his garage and wanting to avoid arguing with yet another teenager after raising his own—had added two eyes to the wall of calendars on my mother's side of the garage. He drew them on one of the old photos in thick permanent marker. Lashes, eyebrows, and the eyes themselves. Lined up right where two eyes pulling into the garage in a big old Chevy should be, if one pulled in correctly. Russ had even taken an additional step. He'd hung a tennis ball from a line attached to a rafter. When the tennis ball hit the windshield, also lined up right where my eyes should be, I was to stop the car. The tennis ball served as a gentle unspoken reminder to keep me from barreling the car through the calendar pictures, the cupboard, the plaster, and straight into the yard beyond.

If Marty wondered about these additions, or had his own garage memories, he didn't say. He opened the cupboards one by one, reaching to the back of even the topmost shelves for lost items, but he found only old paint cans that Bruce then hauled out to the dumpster.

Marty walked over to a heavy oak dresser with three wide drawers and a trifold of beveled mirrors. "This came from Pa's Mom's house. I remember hauling this thing over here when she died."

I told him to take the piece. He and the cousin, with help from Bruce, carried it to the truck they'd brought. Then, they slid it, wrapped with blankets, into the covered cab and tied everything down with ropes. Bruce and the cousin went into the house for water, but Marty returned to the garage. I puttered with making room for more boxes, but from the corner of my eye I watched him study the calendars. He looked at the yellowed tape with the clinging scraps of pictures and then looked away. For the first time I wondered who'd taped the pictures up, who'd taken this on as a project over many years' time. Each one of the photographs we'd torn down represented an entire month of his family's life. All those days of this being his garage, where he'd lifted weights, where he'd learned to park a car (without the need of additional prompts), where he'd been at home.

Marty continued around the garage, picking up items, putting them back. He noted a few things, like a pickle crock that belonged to his father, and then told me about making pickles—the hot steam from the boiling water, the smell of vinegar lingering in the house for days. There was a plate he recognized from holiday gatherings and other things he said he'd like to have.

"Sure," I said. "Of course." They were items I didn't recognize as coming from my original home. My brother, Bill, busy with other things the day of Marty's visit, was fearful of what I'd let go. Bill, despite never living here, worried I would do exactly this: give away something he wanted or something he remembered from our past. I had promised to call if I was unsure or if Marty desired something that was ours.

Then Marty looked up at the rafters, where plywood covered beams to create storage space. He noticed part of a lamp sticking out and called his cousin over: "Look, there's that old lamp I made in shop." Marty turned to me, "I don't want that, brings me bad memories. That guy flunked me and got me kicked off the wrestling team. Told me I wouldn't amount to anything. Later, I poured concrete for him. Don't know why I did that. And I did a good job for him too."

I was surprised at the question in his voice. I imagined Marty wanted or needed to prove a point when he carefully poured the concrete, to show his mettle and wipe away the teacher's words. His refusal to own the lamp suggested something else though—that the pain still lingered nearly fifty years later.

Which idyllic scene, I wondered, did someone tape to the cupboards the month Marty left the team?

There was a loft area above the breezeway that opened only to the garage. Marty spotted boxes I hadn't noticed. With so much on the ground, after all the hauling from all the rooms, I had never bothered to look up. Impossible as it seemed, I wasn't sure I'd ever noticed this storage space—just a few feet between the ceiling of the breezeway and the roofline.

The two boxes were both labeled with black marker: *Christmas Ornaments*. Marty told me the ornaments could be old and might be worth something. Was it okay if he looked through them?

"Yeah," I told him, "I didn't know they were there." And with just that little line, the air charged—a smidge of excitement crackling between us. Did his noticing and my not noticing mean we'd discover something? Some big find my brother would be glad to hear about?

There'd been some resurgence in the market for frosted glass balls and bells with the bell-drop intact, according to Marty. When I had helped my mother decorate for Christmas in our first home, I dropped many such bells. There was the gentle shatter of fine glass, the little shards of color, and the intact silver bell-drop on our braided rug.

"Why don't you pay attention to what you're doing?" my mother had demanded, shouting over the noisy vacuum cleaner. I didn't tell Marty how many of the baubles he hoped to find I'd broken in my childhood.

We searched for a ladder, eventually finding one on the ground near the windows of my old bedroom. Someone, maybe my brother, had been cleaning the gutters. A line of wet debris, spaced every few feet, extended from the end of the house to where the ladder rested. We hauled it to the garage, each carrying an end, although either one of us could have done it by ourselves. Marty leaned the ladder against the wall. He'd hand the boxes down to me if they weren't too heavy, he said, and then we could open them on the garage floor. Marty pulled the first box forward, felt the bottom, tilted it slightly and then half lifted, half slid the box down, saying: "Be careful of that bottom. I'm not sure how strong it is."

I put the box, the cardboard soft and flimsy, on the ground and reached up for the second. Marty lowered it to me. As I set it down he called, "Uh oh, here's where the bottles went."

"What?"

"The bottles. This is where she must've put 'em."

I suppose I looked confused because he descended and stepped aside. I climbed up and rested against the rungs, folded my arms over the ledge, and peered around the small loft. A sheet of plywood created room for storage. The open garage door provided enough light for me to see past the plywood, the layers of insulation, and into the recesses where the roof met the rafters. Now that the boxes of Christmas ornaments were gone, there were only two lawn chairs left—metal rockers with woven green seats, the plastic weaving duct taped where it had begun to weaken. I recognized them as leftovers from cleaning my grandmother's house years ago. Only those two lawn chairs and, beyond them, an accident scene's worth of empty liquor bottles. The bodies rested every which way. Some, inexplicably, with the caps twisted back on, as if the drinker—my mother I was sure—wanted to exert some final measure of control.

Marty offered a flashlight, but I didn't take it. I could see well enough the plastic quart bottles of vodka, whiskey, and brandy scattered about the loft, many nestled far back into the insulation as if they were sleeping. Vodka bottles predominated. Portions of labels were visible, and I made out the Smirnoff logo, the red and silver detailing against the clear bottles looking like Christmas itself.

I leaned into the wall and gazed in wonder. The bottles, those dead soldiers, lying silent and empty. I wanted an accounting, wanted a book or film to give me the gory details. My mother wouldn't tell. She lived in a nursing home—she wouldn't have access to this memory anymore and wouldn't tell if she did.

Lacking any way to get the truth of the story, I crafted it myself as I balanced on the ladder, fingers tapping the metal of the lawn chair. It seemed clever of my stepfather to build this extra storage area above the breezeway. Breezeway. A word I'd never heard before moving here. It connected the garage and the main house. The walls on the north and south ends were all glass. A room filled with sunshine that we had used for watching TV in the summer and, as it was unheated, for storing coats, boots, and extra casseroles in the winter.

She must have done this during the first years we lived here, after I started high school and before Russ retired from his job as supervisor for one of Milwaukee's large factories. Those initial years of her marriage when Russ, I remembered, had often complained about how drunk my mother could get on just one bottle of beer. I couldn't see her climbing, bottle in hand, to carefully hide her empties in the far reaches of the loft. The ladder would have been too heavy and unwieldy for her to maneuver and its presence would have risked drawing attention. Booze had already made my mother clumsy. In the year before marrying Russ, she'd broken her leg and gotten a black eye in separate falls related to drinking.

I pictured her tossing the bottles, bringing them out from some hiding place after I got on the bus for school, waiting for the sound of air brakes from the next stop down the block to be sure I was gone. I saw her hair mushed flat against her head from sleep, still in pajamas and a housecoat. Or maybe it was afternoon, after a day of drinking alone. This seemed more likely, her backing the car out into the driveway and then standing in the empty garage throwing the bottles. How many tries did it take? Was there a dull thud when the bottles hit plywood? Was there an absence of noise if they landed on insulation, nestling themselves down into the soft material? And what about me with my comings and goings? Did she listen for the sound of the bus bringing me home? Her heart pounding—tongue out and off to one side between her teeth (her usual look when concentrating)—determinedly aiming bottles, hurrying before the bus squealed to a stop at the bottom of the driveway.

This scenario made more sense. Made more sense and brought me back a real memory. Mom's gray Impala parked right outside the garage. Russ coming home from work, asking, "Why couldn't you just put the car in the garage?" Mom saying, "I thought I'd go out again." Russ shaking his head then, his quiet way of not arguing. He'd take her keys, pull her car in, and then maneuver his next to it. No eyeballs or tennis ball necessary.

***

Marty opened the last of the ornament boxes, the other box already behind him: strings of Christmas lights spilling out of it, the colored bulbs bright against the cardboard. "Those need to be tossed, the cords are no good and no one wants those big lights." He squatted on the floor, brown packing tape and a jackknife next to him, and searched through the remaining box, looking for something to save. Right away, I could see this box was his. Silver and gold balls, garland decorated with plastic red berries—nothing Mom and I brought here. Our family went in for smaller items: reindeer that clipped onto branches, those bells he hoped for, and tinsel hung strand by strand. Everything in this box would be from his side. My mother had stayed clear about whose possessions were whose. No mingling of Christmas ornaments, no parking in each other's garage space.

Marty yelled for his cousin. I worried that he'd tell him about the bottles, and my heart started to pound, but he just wanted to show him the box's contents. The bottles were apparently not that big of a deal for him, he was already on to new finds. Bruce walked over with Marty's cousin; they'd been trying to get a swing that Marty had helped his dad make down from a tree. Bruce had been grabbing a screwdriver when Marty called out earlier. Now he climbed up and looked around the loft, "Should I throw them down?"

"I'll do it," I told him.

"No," Bruce said, as I knew he would. He pulled himself over the ledge, and I heard him carefully moving on the plywood. "Hope I don't fall through the ceiling," he called out. Bruce pushed the bottles within easy reach over the ledge for me to pick up and take to the dumpster. When he had to stretch his arms from the plywood out over the insulation to grab others, he flung them as best he could from the back of the loft.

Marty took the items worth salvaging from the ornament box to his truck. I could see him and his cousin lounging against the open hatch, with their arms crossed. They appeared to be laughing, but I could be wrong. I picked up the bottles from where they had landed and brought them, two at a time, to the dumpster. Threw them up and over the eight-foot sides, heard them land on other garbage from the basement, the house, and the garage. I walked back, and Bruce called that there were only a few more. And then: "That's it, that's the last one."

I looked up in time to see a vodka bottle tumble over the side, the red and silver label catching the dusty light. I reached out, caught it, and carried it away.

I'm Sorry

I'm sorry about the time I ate a sandwich in your hospice room while you were dying. A portabello mushroom concoction, juices from roasted vegetables mixed with flavored mayonnaise dripping down to the napkin in my lap. Even worse, I drank a thick, caramelly coffee topped with whipped cream—after scrounging for the extra-wide straw deep in my Panera bag. The noise of those rustling pleasures loud against the other sounds in the room: a televised soccer match that my brother, Bill, watched with the volume down low and the subdued rhythm of the oxygen machine with its unchanging inhales and exhales. Your harsh breathing had finally relaxed, and your heart could remember—for a little longer, anyway—what it was supposed to do.

But here's the thing: I didn't know it was wrong to enjoy food with my mother so close to death. You didn't teach me that, and somehow I missed the obvious—that this was a ham on white bread occasion, or maybe McDonald's if takeout was a must.

It wasn't until the nurse came to check your vitals and gave me a quick, odd look as I took a bite that I understood. My chest tightened, and Bill, his own sandwich in hand said, "I guess it's a weird time to be eating." The nurse, whose mother must have taught her well, said, "Not at all, and there's food in the kitchen if the day gets long." She put her hand to my mother's forehead and wrist, and then moved her blanket aside. "Look at your mom's legs," she said and motioned us over. She pointed out the fading color, the blood pulling back, as all your bodily resources tended to your heart.

Food in the kitchen. That's what our family was about. You were the queen of your stove—a frying pan with meat browning, a pot of potatoes boiling, a saucepan simmering with canned vegetables. The sound of a lid bouncing against a boiling pot was a constant throughout my childhood. All of the food on the table at the same time and still hot. This is a thing I would tell you about if, instead of drinking my coffee, and using the straw to get to the cream dotted with beads of caramel in the bottom of the cup, I pulled a chair to your bed, held your hand, and told stories for the few minutes left to us. Strings of events timed to the mechanical inhalations of the artificial oxygen, celebrations you could take with you wherever you're going.

If only. If only I had enough stories for however many breaths you had remaining. But that would be a different girl, maybe the girl from the photographs I never brought to the nursing home. The staff told us that residents like touches from home, but your shelves remained empty. I purchased a chair for the room and brought clothes when the seasons changed, but the pictures in the albums on my closet shelf were all wrong. The frozen moments contained too much of your backstory: anxiety, depression, addictions. I wanted store-bought frames with their pretend families. I wanted to tell you they were us, to point out relatives we both would have liked better than Trudy with her fine clothes, Uncle John with his roaming hands, or even your own mother with her caustic need to control. I wanted to display stories of an alternate history, one I could share with your favorite nurse and the kind aides. It's the daughter from those photos, not me, that could have held your hand and waited to eat her sandwich somewhere else.

Instead, you spent those last hours alone in your small bed, doing the hard work of dying—your grown children in the same room, but not close. Your wrinkles fell away, and your mouth hung open and dry, except for when I swabbed your lips and tongue with water. My brother watched television while I took notes, already playing out how this sandwich thing would go, how it balanced against the rest of the long afternoon.

I wrote my notes on a new laptop—mine had stopped working the day before. I admit I purchased it at Best Buy after receiving the nurse's call that it was time to come, that you were near the end. I recognize that I'm like my dad in this way—this need to buffer in distance, or at least activity, between event and emotion. I never told you how, a few months after he left us, I'd spot him watching my volleyball games through the window of St. Greg's auditorium, or about the time he appeared at the campground I was staying at with his parents. As if by leaving he gave up rights to an easy relationship with me, to enter an event without preapproval. Or perhaps this once-removed relationship was all he had to offer to either of us. It's the need for distance or distraction I recognize—I could stay in the room with you, but not without a laptop or notebook to separate us.

I wanted to do what good daughters might before you passed—to protect myself from some future guilt or distress about this day. As the afternoon slouched on I moved closer, settled in a chair next to you and held your hand, and I did tell you things I remembered—the way we read together, those triple-layered chocolate birthday cakes you made, how you folded your hands during the Hail Mary each night when I was little. You stood at the foot of my bed with your hands pressed together, palms and fingers flat against each other, trying to set a good example. I tried to keep pace through the Our Father and the Hail Mary, stumbling over words I found difficult—*blessed art thou amongst women*—and lines I didn't understand—*the fruit of thy womb*. My own hands were a lazy fold, fingers woven together, no matter how many times you told me that looked sloppy.

I called your brother and had him talk to your unresponsive ear, let him make whatever peace he found necessary and say his goodbyes. The earlier crinkling of the Panera bag and the empty coffee cup betrayed me though, revealed me. The loud noise and the pleasing food in the death room exposed the dissonance between my studied actions and who I really am, and I'm sorry for that. Sorry I didn't hold your hand earlier and say I'd miss you. Sorry I didn't feel worse.

When your heart stopped, Bill and I were sitting

beside you, touching you. We waited a long time for an inhale that wouldn't come. The oxygen machine continued though. Carried on its useless rhythm until we reached over to shut it off.

Just Leave the Damn Thing Open

Our neighbors keep an extra house key on a hook in their garage. My father's is also on a hook—inside his shed, to the left of the door. During my childhood, Grandma kept her spare buried in a flowerpot. And, as an adult, I hid my mother's key in a broken downspout next to her garage. After it disappeared, I put a new one under a planter in the window box.

My husband and I switched to a coded lock because our daughters kept telling everyone where to find our keys. Now they tell everyone the combination. The original plan was to update the code frequently, but we lost the instructions and haven't reprogrammed since we installed the darn thing. Some days I can't think to say the numbers in the right order and stand on the back porch, grocery bags balanced against my hip, and rely on my fingers to remember the pattern. So far it's all worked out. I always manage to make my way in; my fear of being left outside comes to nothing.

***

After my father left, my mother started locking the door. No more returning from errands to find an aunt napping in the living room or watching *As the World Turns*. No more coming home from school—all sixth-grade hungry—to find Grandma had stopped by to leave a plate of cookies on the counter. Now people called first or left notes in the door. *When will you be home?*

My mother, despite her insistence on the lock, struggled with our new routines. She'd stand on the porch—tongue stuck between her teeth—bags of canned goods, meat, and potatoes balanced against the steps and call to the key hiding in her handbag, "Oh, come on now." A prayer more than a command, *oh, come on now*, called to tight jar lids, a splinter stuck in a hand, nail files, and stockings that went missing.

On school days, I came home first and unlocked the house before Mom returned from her factory job at Briggs and Stratton. The wrecked screen door was bowed from the push of my hand—the small squares of fine metal weave patterned against my skin—and torn from where I dragged my new hardware-store key over the mesh, liking the zipper sound and the way the dust sprinkled down to the porch. The door bounced against me as I turned the key in the back lock, chanting *righty tighty, lefty loosey* before greeting the dog and stepping into the silent kitchen. At night, dishes washed and dried, Mom, with her own set of car, garage, and house keys on a small ring wrapped around her finger, escaped to the tavern up the block. Her real ring, a wedding ring, slept in her top bedroom drawer. My father slept in a new apartment with a new woman.

***

A drop of nail polish, like red for the house and pink for the car, would have done it. Or those fitted fobs for around the top of the keys. We could even have paid extra for printed patterns—Green Bay Packer motifs are popular in this area—although this option wasn't available in the early 1970s. Any of these solutions could have eliminated the wasted time spent sorting through handbags for keys. One lucky thing, though—there weren't as many keys back then. We didn't have boats, or campers, or second homes to keep locked. People in my neighborhood didn't have office keys; the dads were laborers and the moms stayed home with the kids. Well, that isn't completely true. My mother worked for Mr. Gibbons on Tuesday nights as a key punch operator when my father still lived at home.

Since Mom worked after regular business hours, she had her own key to his small office on 27th Street. Usually I went with her and while she typed I sat at a big green desk doing math problems or playing with Barbie dolls. My brothers, both teenagers then, were at football practice or their own jobs. If she had to work past eight, Mom left me at home.

"Why can't you just take her with you?" my father asked each time she put her coat on to leave.

Most nights my father worked in the garage on his Model A Ford or watched TV in the basement. On Tuesdays though, he talked on the telephone in our kitchen. He used a low, even voice that sounded unfamiliar to me. I wanted to be near him and looked for reasons to come into the kitchen so I could watch the way he moved, the long spiral of the phone cord following him from table to counter as he paced. The only familiar thing about him was the way his hand—the one not cradling the phone—crossed his chest, his bottle of Pabst held steady against his heart. One night, I started to unload the dishwasher while he talked.

"Never mind, I'll do it," he told me in the sweet voice, cupping his hand over the receiver. "You go read now." He kept talking, opened the top of the dishwasher and gently put away each dish. A first, as far as I knew, listening from around the corner in the hallway, the dog held tight in my lap. I wondered what my older brothers would make of this soft-spoken dad finishing my chores. The dad we knew treated the vintage cars in his garage with tenderness, but with family his anger rose sharply and startling.

I want to say I was too young to understand his tête-à-tête. But that doesn't ring true. I didn't tell my mother about the dishwasher. On the other hand, she didn't ask what we did those evenings she worked and didn't question why he wanted me with her. Besides, she should have known. Grandma always told her that wives belonged home at night.

***

One middle school summer I traveled with cousins from Milwaukee to Winona, Minnesota, to attend the funeral of a great-great aunt none of us had ever met. My grandmother also came, although in a different car. My mother stayed home. Long car rides made her nervous.

Over coffee and crumb cake the day we arrived,

the Winona relatives worried about Aunt Laura's possessions. There were rumors of treasures in the house, even hidden money. Laura had been a childless recluse, subject to all sorts of stories due to her independent state, and nobody knew for sure. Once lawyers got involved no one would get anything—that seemed the consensus among the in-town family members.

On the day of the funeral, Grandma and a Milwaukee aunt took me to visit Laura's house—a graying Victorian where she'd lived alone until a few days before her death. In the spirit of *seize the day*, after promising me no one would mind our keyless entry, they pushed aside layers of leaves and cobwebs to lower me through an unlocked basement window.

Inside, framed sepia photographs of hat-wearing men and big-bosomed women watched as I shouted up my findings: straight-back chairs piled against a wall, tables dusty with rows of mason jars, boxes of dishes, the cardboard sinking into itself. I had to weave amongst the boxes and push through spider webs to find the stairs. In a corner, near the sump pump, a shadowed double sink and wringer washer machine lurked, something I recognized from years back in my grandmother's basement. I feared Aunt Laura would appear, look out from one of the ornate mirrors leaning against the walls and beckon to me, or hiss her displeasure at my intrusion into her home.

When I came up from the basement, I could see my grandmother peering in through the parlor's windowpane. She cupped her face with her hands against the glass and scanned the room until she spotted me. As I moved through the inside, feet clomping against the hardwood floors, dust motes guiding my way, Grandma walked along the outside of the house, stopping at each window to follow my progress—my Milwaukee aunt a shadow behind her. Concern for my safety didn't propel Grandma over the weedy, uneven lawn; no, she knew what she wanted. I was now worthy of suspicion. She carefully watched my steps until I opened the door. All of us ready to inherit.

***

This is about the lack of a key. My empty hand and empty pockets the afternoon my mother, purse dangling from her forearm, came up the sidewalk to greet me as I returned from an overnight with friends. She was going out dancing and had already locked up. On Sunday afternoons, the VFW post often hosted polka bands. "I should," she said, "stay outside on such a nice day."

That's true; it was a nice day. I remember the blue sky frozen like a strip of watercolor behind the neighbor's trees and chimney, the expanding and receding sound of Mr. Marimonti's lawn mower next door, the way he walked towards us and then away. I'm sure I nodded and shrugged my shoulders, certain I'd get in. My mother could be unpredictable. I hadn't a clue what time she'd return or why she'd locked me out.

But I couldn't find a way in—no keys hidden in the usual spots, and my bedroom window sealed tight. I walked to the park and the store and then, worst of all, waited for her. I sat on the front porch, the gray paint peeling from the pockmarked stairs, the dog watching from her comfortable spot inside, atop the living room couch. Once, when my heart began to race, I got a ball out of the garage. The solid rubber ball in my hand a comfort, each loud thunk against the steps a prayer she'd return soon. My steady rhythm, the imaginary crowd cheering, and the dog lifting her head to track the ball eventually calmed me.

I had friends in the neighborhood, but on a Sunday afternoon—family day—I refused to risk looking odd and alone at their doors, their mothers sighing as they let me in. I didn't yet recognize my own appearance gave me away. That the sleeves falling above my wrist bones, the dark shadows under my eyes, and my short hair at a time of braids or ponytails told the world everything they needed to know, long before my mother walked into a room without a wedding ring on her hand.

So I played games against the porch, chasing the ball into the neighbor's yard if it flew off on an unexpected trajectory. He had a weeping willow tree I longed to nap under, its huge branches curving down to the ground—a hidden cave—sunlight filtering through the slender leaves. My parents hated the willow; its map of roots worked their way between our cement basement blocks until spindly roots grew along our walls, thin red shoots looking for something.

I knew better than to call my father or grandmother. If I complained about my mother, told about being locked out for example, I might be taken away. Put in someone else's care. Even then, I understood the comfort of the familiar.

My mother returned toward evening. She asked

how I was and I answered, "Fine." She asked what I'd done all day and I said, "Nothing." I walked away from her then, having found my own key for locking her out.

***

My mother had a goodbye ritual before going out for the evening. Her voice would become distracted, her attention already somewhere else. She'd blot her red lipstick with toilet paper and then admonish, "Don't open the door for anyone." Such a stupid saying—as if this ensured protection for me or absolution for her. Her real concern was that I not let my father in if, as I knew she hoped, he showed up.

On those nights she went out, my focus was to listen for her return, praying for a release from the awful waiting. Once she returned, my anxiety lessened, but the night wore on. I'd steady her as she staggered to her bedroom where, once settled, she'd watch TV with the volume on high. Across the hall, I lay awake calculating when she'd fall asleep. I wanted that TV off. Only then would I believe the night finished. A foolish girl, I wasn't content to put cotton in my ears and leave well enough alone. If I simply snuck in and lowered the sound, she'd know I had touched her television; if I turned it off she assumed she was responsible. I risked the click of that on/off button, her waking to see me at the foot of the bed, and the night becoming even longer.

***

An end table with attached magazine rack sat next to the breezeway couch and to the side of the back door that led to the kitchen of my stepfather's house. As far as I could tell, magazines had never been stored there before we moved in, and we didn't store magazines there afterwards. The top of the end table usually held current and past flyers for Kohl's or Sentry, or the department stores my parents favored, Boston Store and Sears. The magazine rack held extra keys for the back door—which we only locked at bedtime. "Did you lock the door?" Our way of saying good night to each other, an important ritual despite the fact, it occurs to me, that all of those keys remained right outside the door.

***

My mother was in her eighties, living alone, when I first hid her car keys to keep her from driving. While she napped in the back bedroom, I walked around and around her rooms searching for a hiding spot, fearful she'd guess any location I chose. Eventually I settled on a yellow two-quart casserole with a lid. She never found them, although she did have the car towed to the dealership to be rekeyed.

"I knew you were home," I told my mother over the phone one evening. I had stopped during my lunch hour to check on her—something I tried to do weekly. I knocked on the heavy breezeway door and then on the kitchen's cloudy picture window, but she never answered.

"How do you know? You should call first," my mother replied. I reminded her she often ignored the phone, and then—without thinking—I blurted that her dog told me. It ran barking between the kitchen window and the bedroom hallway if she was home and stared quietly from its bed next to the stove if she was gone. We laughed about it, but the next week when I came to visit the curtains were closed tight—the dog now unseen and unheard.

***

Several months ago, we repainted our kitchen. The window above the sink remains bare and I doubt we'll get around to hanging a curtain, blind, or swag anytime soon. The days pass too swiftly for our attention to land on this detail. As it is, the view of our yard, absent a window covering, has become familiar, even soothing. There is a tree-lined fence at the end of the lot line and, beyond that, the county highway flows with a constant hum of travel. I lock the doors when I'm working in my basement office, but my loved ones know how to get in.

I still wait for the release certain sounds bring—the garage opening, the door handle turning. Signals of safe arrivals. And always, there is the need for things to be finished: the kitchen clean, the television off, the daughters settled. The Hail Marys whispered to a dark and quiet room.

Every Action
a Memory

I woke early, the night not quite all the way gone,
on a Saturday with little planned. A calm spot in the
holiday rush—my husband, our daughters, and the
dogs still asleep. I moved through the house pulling
back curtains, raising blinds, and feeling blue and
restless on an ashen day. We were still a week out
from the solstice, but it already felt like midwinter—
the sun wouldn't rise much above the tree line behind
our house before it turned back again.

Every action brought back memories. Stirring hot
oatmeal over the stove reminded me of rolling out
cookies and my grandmother's long, slow days of
baking. The warm smell of her oven, the soft click
as the gas flamed on and off, nothing rushed—no
tension in the hands sprinkling colored sugar over
rows of cut-out Santas, stars, and reindeer.

Pouring coffee, wrapping my hands around the hot
mug, and holding my face to the steam, I conjured
my mother. All the weekend mornings of my childhood she'd lounge at the kitchen table wearing

her nightgown with the brown and blue paisley housecoat over it. She'd prop her heavy head—hair uncombed—in her left hand, and caress the Currier & Ives coffee cup, purchased with Green Stamps from the grocers in her right.

Another memory returned as I sipped my coffee. This one of Mom in the basement of our house on Milwaukee's south side, shaking out our plastic Christmas tablecloth. I heard the snap as she settled it over the table made of plywood and sawhorses my father and brothers had created for her. She'd let me iron the napkins while she built up the dining room scene from scraps, readying our house for a party. She smoothed the plastic tablecloth, wrinkled from being folded for a year, flat against the wood and added a freshly washed red table runner to the end reserved for adults. The tree-shaped salt and pepper shakers were found in the bottom of the last possible box scavenged from the attic, and she filled each one over the sink before letting me arrange them on the table runner. We talked about the pies my grand-mother would bring and who'd make a Jell-O mold. I wondered aloud who'd bring me gifts and she said, "It's best not to get too excited. You'll only be disap-pointed."

My mother's words followed me through that long day of preparation, and like a wash applied to a photograph, dulled all other images. Even smudged, my view of her: dressed up for my father's arrival home from work, her soft gray angora with random splashes of white circles, her red lipstick painted on bright and perfect. She hung tinsel while she waited for him, first one strand, and then another, each placed just-so over the branches of our double balsam. Even that reminiscence comes with a shadow: her sharp words like slaps when my brothers or I tossed the silver strands in the air to watch them float and settle over the tree. "Stop that," she'd say. "Why can't you do anything nice?"

***

It's nearly Christmas, my first one without a mother. There is a new emptiness to the season, although I can't say I miss her. It's been years since she snapped a tablecloth in the air or filled a table with pretty things and her home cooking. Years since we planned a celebration together. Eventually, she preferred to spend holidays, as well as most other days, alone—sleeping or reading the newspaper.

As I'm pouring more coffee, my eldest brother, Bill, calls. He says he feels scattered, that he keeps sending holiday packages to our alcoholic brother, Steven, up in the northern armpit of the state. Bill's not sure why he does this. Can't figure out why he packs the flat-rate box from the post office full of gifts, even adding canned peaches he finds on sale at the Piggly Wiggly.

I know why Bill does this, though it's just like him to claim that there's no reason beyond a two-for-one sale at the grocery store. He doesn't think Steven, with his jaundiced skin and belly distended from liver failure, will have another Christmas. So he's getting everything done now, covering all his bases, keeping himself busy—and doubtless not even remembering all those bowls of peaches we ate for dessert as kids.

Mom divided the canned peaches equally between

our three bowls. Any remainders went to me because I was the girl, or to Bill because he was the eldest. We were supposed to cut each rubbery length of peach into chunks instead of shoving entire slices into our mouths, but the pieces were slippery and sometimes shot out of the dish and onto the floor for the dog to scarf down. Steven liked putting a slice sideways between his lips and making a yellow smile. Bill and I always cracked up laughing, and eventually our dad yelled at us to stop messing around. Soon, someone got smacked upside the head and we would finish the meal in silence. Maybe canned peaches in winter would provide something like home to Steven, spark some forgotten connection that could save him.

Bill tells me he opened the Bible yesterday, turned to Proverbs, and found the perfect verse to settle himself. He thinks this is eerie. I tell him it's the universe speaking, giving him what he needs. "Maybe," he says.

When I ask which proverb he found, he can no longer remember. I wonder if the universe is telling him to look elsewhere for answers, but I keep this to myself. Instead I tell him I feel lonesome.

"I guess that's it," Bill says.

"Yeah," is all I can think to reply.

Both of us have houses full of people and things to do. Yet here we are on this cold, empty day, both wanting something in the past, a return to our places at the kitchen table. Bill sitting across from Mom; Steven and me on either side of Dad. On the table a bowl of mashed potatoes creamy with milk and butter, mushy green beans from a can, a beef roast carved into thin slices, salt and pepper, more butter.

This is what I want anyway—though not for long. Just for an instant I want to feel us all together again. All at one table before our father has the affair, our parents' divorce, and our mother starts drinking. I want a do-over of our family life: this time the dad doesn't have a temper or hit, the mom doesn't cry or take pills, the kids don't have tummy aches from the stress of it all. Nobody spills milk.

***

Bill gets off the phone to mail his flat-rate box of t-shirts, deer sausage, and those peaches to Steven. I go for a walk. I consider mailing a box, measure how that would feel—how it will feel when he leaves us if I don't send one. Then I shake my head. How stupid. I'm not sending a damn box.

I walk through woods a half mile from our house, breaking through a thin crust of icy snow near the Bark River. A Wood Duck swims up the current, all drab, dreary browns until I look again, catch the slight green shimmer of her back and the soft white coloring around her dark eyes.

Usually I see other people out on this trail jogging or walking their dogs, but today everything is still. I don't spot deer moving among the bare trees or flush other birds out with my approach. A few last oak leaves decorate the path—leftovers from a windy night—but mostly the snow is undisturbed until I crunch through, my boots ruining the pristine, flat whiteness extending through the woods. A duck startles as I draw closer and flies up, but she soon settles in the water again and seems happy enough, heading upstream on this cold, gray day.

The truth is I can't return to the pretend warmth of that long-ago kitchen any more than the duck will ever be in the same stream twice. The longing, that loneliness I mentioned to my brother, has always been more about a desire to leave than a need to stay.

Things That Won't Happen Again

I'm washing my brother's dishes. Actually, I'm boiling his flatware before I can begin the washing. It's all that dirty: the knives and spoons coated with something filmy, the fork tines clogged with what looks like old eggs. Other than the jarring sounds of pans sliding against pans as I look through cupboards or move dishes from counter to sink, the cabin is utterly quiet, the heavy air undisturbed.

My brother, Steven—bearded, thin, and haggard enough to appear Christ-like—says he might have barfed in the sink, but he's not sure. He mentions this from the one comfortable chair in his cabin, where he sits naked from the waist down, cigarettes and vodka within easy reach, his long hands flat on the black leather armrests, and his body motionless as he stares out the sliding glass doors to the woods beyond his deck. Steven's golden retriever, her fur dull and matted, lies on the rug next to his chair. The dog doesn't bark, or wag her tail, but tracks my movements with her eyes.

The nakedness is fair. Steven's stomach is so distended from his failing liver that all his pants are useless. Besides, he didn't expect my visit. I've arrived without invitation, after driving on winter roads for several hundred miles, to see if he's still alive.

***

In our last telephone conversation, Steven's voice was low and full of pauses. He described shooting pains in his chest, how little he ate, and how much he slept. While I drove, I prayed the reason he hadn't answered his phone for the last several days was because it wasn't charged, or because he was sleeping a lot, lost in the wild-colored dreams he'd been telling me about.

Both assumptions were correct. I discovered this when I walked into his cabin, as casual as some neighbor with a coffee cake, although it was chicken and rice I'd brought to cook for him. When I called his name he didn't move from the chair, greet me, or rush to cover himself. He just said, "I'm not going to some damn hospital."

And I, shutting the door behind me, childishly replied, "No one asked you to."

I've messed up before, arguing or trying to reason. Or, worst of all, using my social worker skills—something he always detected and mocked me for—to get him to stop drinking, to change who he'd become. Even now, way into my forties, I'm only the younger sister, and anything I suggest is unlikely to happen. Instead, I'll boil the flatware and wash all the dishes, because nothing is clean and I want to make him a meal. It's unlikely the dishes will get dirty again once I leave, not with how used-up Steven looks, not after his admission that nothing stays down anymore except for vodka.

This is what I'm here for, at least in part. With my grandmother and mother dead, it's become my job to make a last attempt to save, or at least feed, my brother. I remember us eating meals together, the pancakes our grandmother made: the smell of bacon, the eggs fried in butter in a cast iron skillet. Our own mother always at the stove, making meat and potatoes and a vegetable each night. After supper the two of us would do the dishes together. Steven washing and me up on a stool drying each plate and putting it away in the cupboard where it belonged. I want to give this to him one more time, to change the air in the horrible cabin, cover the cigarette smoke, the unbathed-body and dirty-dog smell, to change it into something like home—like our grandmother's home. Like the people we were.

Steven knows this, I'm sure of it. There's the way he mentions the sound of the chicken frying, and the way he sniffs the air as I turn the meat over in the skillet. I serve him such a small portion, resisting the urge to cut the meat for him. Slowly he eats everything on the plate, being precise about each bite, and looking almost happy by the time he finishes. He tells me how good it tastes, but soon after he pushes heavily on the arms of his recliner to stand and make his way to the bathroom, and I doubt he'll reheat the leftovers I've wrapped and put in the refrigerator.

Steven returns out of breath, with a towel wrapped around him. He tells me, "Don't go in there." I pull up a hard kitchen chair and sit next to the table piled with weeks of mail. I'd much rather scrub at spots on the counter, or vacuum around the dog, but I'm remembering that Bible story, the one about Martha and Mary hanging out with Jesus, how Martha cleans while Mary listens. I realize I'm imitating the wrong sister and I'll regret this, so I stop and sit down. It's clear to me I won't visit Steven here again. Not with how large his belly has become on his emaciated body or the way he's missing his ankles, his lower legs just swollen, jaundiced blobs ending in feet. One foot, I notice, has dried poop stuck to it. I point this out and he expresses minimal interest, just moves his head unhurriedly to look and says he doesn't know if it is his or the dog's. He does not attempt to clean himself. Still, I press where his ankle should be, and comment on how long the skin takes to bounce back. There are lines on both legs, streaks of ochre against his skin's oddly yellow-tan color, like the straight roads on a map. I realize they represent past bouts of diarrhea, but this time I stay quiet.

Despite the gravity, the finality of this visit, my heart isn't pounding and my thoughts aren't all jumbled and rubbery as often happens to me in a crisis. It's more like the lingering cigarette smoke is a fog I must wade through to cross to the chair and sit facing Steven. I fight the desire to pull back, to dissociate and watch the events play out from the ceiling somewhere or out in the woods—the woods my brother loved. I'm surprised by the memory of a phone call from months, even a year, ago. He was sitting on his deck, tossing a ball to the dog—and drinking, from the sound of his voice. I was busy running errands and told him so. He mocked me and called me foolish for living my suburban life driving my van, doing everything from a list, and eating eggs only at breakfast.

"That's what you're doing. I know that's what you're doing," Steven accused from his sunny patio. My stunned silence as I drove the curved roads of my neighborhood encouraged him to ramble on. He said that I could eat anything, anytime—there were no rules. His words were sarcastic, his laughter cruel.

***

If I keep working, if I vacuum, as my mother surely would, perhaps I'll make up for the chicken, do something right. There is a risk to just sitting with each other, not even a sink of dirty dishes between us. What if I say something wrong, open some old wound between us, and there is never another time to fix it? Never another time to reiterate, restate, re-anything.

I talk about my kids, ask questions about his dog, the best things he's ever done, and about his worst memory ever. Without a pause, he tells about when he was a kid, seven or so, and I was a baby. He was in the garage with our dad and Todd Markowski from down the block who smoked smelly cigars. Steven sat in the driver's seat of one of the old cars our Dad loved to restore. I imagine Steven's pride, how big his chest felt, at hanging with the men. I can see the way his brown hair stood up in the back, his freckled face with its slanted smile, one side up, one side down. As Steven talks, he doesn't look at me but out the screen window, at the spot between the pines where the deer come in the early evening. Steven tells how he was supposed to press the brake pedal so Dad could show Mr. Markowski something. Of course he messed up—what little boy wouldn't?—pushed the gas pedal instead and caused some problem. Maybe the men jumped back, startled at the sound of the motor racing, or maybe the car lurched forward, Steven doesn't say. But he tells about the swearing and name-calling that came next, all in front of Mr. Markowski who kept smoking his cigar. Steven refused to go into the garage after that. Never, no matter how much our father asked.

As I unroll Steven's story, I add bottles of Pabst to the workbench underneath the windows facing the backyard, and a smack as he's hauled out by his elbow, the harsh words condemning him, ringing from him, as he runs to his room and slams his door. Refusing, even at that age, to let anyone see his tears. Or, it's possible he sat frozen in the lousy cab of the broken car intent, despite the shouting, on the view of crab apple trees, wash lines, and our white house with its red shutters outside the double glass of windshield and windows. Intent on the shadow of our mother moving past a window, carrying the new sister he wasn't allowed to touch without cleaning up first.

In truth, I'm not sure about the back wall of the garage, if there really were windows or if Steven only stared at the tool bench with its litter of car parts and amber bottles of beer. The wall covered with a pegboard of hooks for hammers and saws, their ghostly outlines drawn with magic marker, and shelves with jars of nails and screws all meticulously labeled and cared for.

After he tells his story Steven turns to me and asks, "What you gonna do, write about it?" I remain silent, make no promises, already wondering how to memorize each portion of this day, how it might look on the page. I fear I'll forget his sunken cheeks and ragged beard, or the way he lifts his unlit cigarette to his mouth inhaling and exhaling nothing. The drawn-out pace of his words, the raspy sound of his laugh, his light touch on my arm, and even the long imprint of my finger on his ankle make me wish for paper, some way to get it all outside myself.

His dog cries at the door and I take her outside. Tail up, she checks the air and tests the length of her leash while I pour corn for the deer from a bucket in the shed. I'm on Steven's property, his land ends where the Chequamegon-Nicolet National Forest begins, but it's the crab apple trees in the backyard of our parents' home I'm picturing. Steven had an ability to lean against a rake, motionless for long periods of time. Mom and I would watch him from the kitchen window, her hand holding back the ruffled curtain so we could both see. I remember her exasperation at his lack of progress. How she'd say, "That kid ... What'll become of that kid?" I knew I could rake better, get rid of all the crab apples and make her happy if only I were big enough.

Later, as I drive away from his cabin, another memory returns. I'm still little, and Steven has asked me to toss a football with him. Crab apples and yellow leaves litter the autumn ground. Our laundry line posts denote end zones. There are the rich sounds of crackling leaves and pigskin hitting palms as he teaches me to catch and pass. He plays defense and I make my slow way towards those laundry pole goal posts. Success is in the air, as he allows me to get close, oh so close, to a touchdown. And then he uses all his power to push me back to the fifty-yard line and tackle me until time is finally called and the game is over.

Driving south towards home I suppose Steven is in his chair, the dog stretched out beside him. They'll both watch for deer making their way out of the woods at dusk looking for corn. Later Steven will rouse himself enough to pour another drink or light a cigarette. I'll futz with the car's radio or talk on my cell phone. Both of us are moving on.

Riptides

Not long ago, vacationing in Costa Rica with my husband and daughter, I met a woman on the hotel shuttle that took tourists to the ocean. Her youngest, she told me, got caught up in a riptide earlier in the week. The little girl flailed, unable to touch bottom, afraid in the strong swells, and the lifeguards rescued her. Now the entire sea was suspect—she refused to return, refused to chance swimming anymore.

***

At the beach there were postings about the unpredictable, strong pulls of water known as rip currents and their gentle, sun-and-moon-influenced misnomer, riptides. The signs identified rips as dangerous and advised precautions. As with most things, the narrative confirmed, it's best not to struggle or panic. Swim slant to save yourself or tread water and signal for help. Fighting only leads to exhaustion, to being carried farther and farther away, the odds of successful rescue decreasing with distance. Stay close to shore is what it all meant to me, close enough not to risk panic or losing each other.

In the ocean, I tried to keep my daughter in front of me, near enough to touch, ignoring her desire to swim beyond my reach. Even with the posters, I couldn't discern what the lifeguards easily recognized: the broken wave pattern, the line of churning debris, or the unexpected calm that indicated peril. I decided if the phantom sea reached for us, I'd grab her and pull her to safety—anything to keep her from vanishing, from leaving me.

A good plan as long as I was in charge. However, minutes after my spouse replaced me so I could warm up, a rip current was spotted and the crowds of swimmers called in. Everyone except my husband and daughter returned to the beach and wrapped themselves in sun-warmed towels to wait for the risk to pass. My family soon became the objects of frantic lifeguard whistling. Just as I stood, ready to go to them—the shuttle woman's story now my own, her child's face transposed onto my mine—they noticed the empty water, the harried commotion onshore, and waded towards me. Both still smiled, unconcerned about my worry, unconcerned that I had imagined my daughter in distress, calling for help, lost. Unable to find me.

***

If more than an hour had passed since lunch we could swim in Connie's pool. Never for long, though—inevitably someone tattled about a dunking, splashed the hanging laundry, or woke the sleeping baby. *Find something else to do,* threatened as we climbed the ladder back out of the pool, *or I'll find something for you.*

We—Connie, Lisa from across the alley, and I—
lived to sunbathe on the front sidewalk. Bath towels
or no, our swimsuits, thighs, and pillowed arms left
liquid Rorschachs. Too impatient to stay still for
long, we rowed our towels down the dry stream of
pavement, leaving less and less of our damp selves
behind as we traveled the five houses from Connie's
to mine. If we didn't put down a towel on the sand-
colored cement, fine gravel and dirt clung to our
arms and legs and needed rinsing off with the hose.
Sometimes a water fight ensued, and the cycle began
all over again.

On sweltering days, steam rose from our wet
shadows when we stood, the condensation becoming
another self after our mothers called us in to peel
potatoes or set the table. We aimed for dry swimsuits before supper, ever hopeful of wearing them all
through the meal. This was what we wanted at the
age of eight or nine: to know there'd be more time—
that the trap of indoors hadn't closed on us. A swim-
suit during the meal meant we could eat and get
back outside, that we'd escaped the directive: *Take
that dripping thing off. You're done for the day.*

***

We beached ourselves in the middle of the sidewalk
one long afternoon after another. Our neighbor lady,
Mrs. Marimonto, stepped around us if she ambled by
on her way home from Schmidt's corner market. "No,
no," she'd insist when we offered to move. "You kids
stay there."

Now I wonder, what if Mrs. Marimonto was a secret
anthropologist for the city of Milwaukee? What

might she have read in the silhouettes left behind when we ran inside to beg for popsicles or Kool-Aid? Could she see my frequent tummy aches, some echo of the constant yelling in my house? Would the pressure points of Connie's thin arms indicate beatings? Did Lisa's hips already look uneven from her lopsided stance, one sibling after another balanced on her young bones? But Mrs. Marimonto, an ordinary housewife, simply walked past, and we stayed on our towel rafts, soaking in the sidewalk's warmth against the chlorine coolness from Connie's pool. That safe, paralyzing pavement. We were visible from every neighbor's window, beyond harm from the outside, and all adventures ended at the street corner.

***

Hidden undertows connect these scenes—concealed threats I couldn't control or adequately name. The signs just not clear enough. In the working-class neighborhood of my childhood the indoor swells of our parents' dissatisfactions and angers were the most dangerous. The problems—broken appliances, disobedient children, and unexpected bills—often played out during supper with raised voices and smacks to the head. It was the reason we wanted to avoid hearing: *You're done for the day.* Our own voices unheard, our imaginary power stripped away, like some ongoing riptide that refuses to weaken.

***

None of us knew how to read our parents' signals any better than I could spot a change in the surf. A deceptive smoothness the worst of all, trouble rushing in on all sides, dampening the lesser waves of daily setbacks. Summer afternoons though, we could drift along on our own—until our watery doppelgangers dried into the very air we breathed, and our real selves pushed off the sidewalks, grabbed our towels, and went inside at suppertime. Those restless twins wanted to disappear and become something else, but our mothers kept calling us back to their lonely houses. Now, far from Milwaukee, I can better name what resembled anger as fear. Their need, I assume, for a lifesaving interruption to days of sameness. That cold dread of the child leaving and the adults left to fend for themselves.

We—Connie, Lisa, and I—must have sensed another way out, realized if you made a raft of your body and floated the difficult current would eventually weaken. You could reach another shore on your own. As long as you didn't look back, didn't let the anxious flailing arms call you in.

The Hallway in My House

This is about our hallway, a birthday party, the socks I wore in high school, and—although less than I initially thought—my daughter. Mostly it's about fitting in.

First the hallway. My fourteen-year-old, Polly, and I sat in the snug upstairs hallway of our two-story colonial. The rest of the household—Polly's dad and her ten-year-old sister—were already asleep. Polly pushed her shoulders and blonde head against one wall and bent her legs to drum the other wall with her toes. I sat cross-legged, chin resting on hands, elbows resting on knees, and resisted telling her to get her feet off my walls. I wondered if my expression was like hers: stunned, with a mixture of confusion. As if we'd witnessed something mortifying and now needed peace and quiet, a chance to come home to ourselves, to combobulate—if combobulate is really a word—in this spot of a hallway.

But we hadn't been to some prodigious event, some tragic or comedic happening. All we'd done was drive together from one part of Waukesha County to another. A couple of hours earlier, I had left our home in Hartland, Wisconsin, and drove twenty minutes to Wales to pick Polly up from her friend Jessica's birthday party. Polly being the unfortunate age in which her desire to be with me was small but her need of me—not old enough to drive or have friends who drive—remained great.

***

The birthday party was at Jessica's new house. Polly hadn't mentioned that, and I mistakenly began driving to where Jessica's party had been held the previous year, a grand place in the upscale Hawksnest subdivision with its circles and courts of traditional Georgian Colonials, Early American Tudors, and faux-French Manor Houses, all with requisite cedar shake roofs.

I knew my way through Hawksnest. Polly had befriended a different girl from there back in preschool. The mom, Liz, and I often talked outside the classroom while the girls sang the goodbye song and packed up their bags. One day, Liz invited us over for a play date and we followed her home. Her Toyota minivan led my Dodge minivan into a neighborhood that I'd assumed was a shortcut to her house.

My husband and I had lived in the area only since I'd become pregnant with Polly. After her birth, my focus revolved around the blocks of our small subdivision and trips to the local Piggly Wiggly for groceries. It wasn't until Liz didn't just pass through, but turned off Windrush Circle and continued up the long drive leading to her house that I felt like I was finally, foolishly, waking up to the community around me. Liz's home had an acre of perfect grass for a lawn, a sculpted rock garden, and variegated green shrubbery that emphasized new construction. I realized I wouldn't simply drive past the local McMansions while raising a family in Hartland; I would stop for coffee, drop the kids off, make new friends.

I'd never been in a house so different from my own. A house with so much distance between sandwiches in the kitchen and dessert in the living room, and where children played out of sight—and hearing— in their own toy room. We finished eating and then walked a long way to the swing set at the end of the yard. Liz and I toted glasses of iced tea with lemon wedges and juice boxes for the kids while they ran ahead with sand buckets and shovels.

I watched the girls when Liz hiked back for something she'd forgotten. All of this foreign from the play dates at my house where friends and I sipped coffee at my kitchen table while the kids goofed around outside, close by and visible through the screened patio doors. Once Liz returned, I feigned interest in the discussion about locations for an in-ground pool. While we debated the merits of a diving board vs. a slide, I kept an ear on Polly's conversation, fearful she'd comment on the differences in our homes or ask why her toys didn't reside in a room of their own.

***

Polly had to redirect me on our drive to Jessica's party. I fussed at her about the route and asked why Jessica's family had moved. Polly could only tell me they'd wanted something larger, something near a golf course because Jessica played for the high-school team. One phone call to my husband to check the forgotten address later and only moderately frustrated with each other, we eventually found Jessica's house. She now lived in a new subdivision, The Legends of Brandybrook. We drove through the narrow entrance and down a long drive to what looked to be a castle on a hill—that castle turned out to be the homeowners' association's club. Across the street from the clubhouse was a swimming pool with a huge spiral slide peeking out from behind the fence, multiple tennis courts, and a building with exercise equipment visible through smoky glass. On the perfect expanse beyond, grand houses lined streets that spidered out from a golf course.

Jessica's new house was close to the swimming pool and across the street from the golf course. I dropped Polly off at the top of the circle drive and—no longer welcome to walk in with her—watched her knock on the beveled glass door. A mom greeted her, took the package from her hand (a gift that now looked small and poorly wrapped), waved in the direction of my latest Dodge minivan, and ushered Polly into the house. In-ground automatic sprinklers spritzed on as I drove away, a signal that the activities would all be indoors and even the front yards would maintain their fairway green.

***

When I returned several hours later, I had on black sweatpants and the blue Sky Chefs Catering t-shirt that I slept in, my typical dress for nights in our neighborhood. I assumed Polly would run to the van.

Unfortunately, the party ran late. I walked up to the porch, rang the doorbell, and listened as gongs sounded throughout the mansion. Jessica's mom, Karen, invited me in and I joined other parents on pick-up duty already gathered in the foyer. She soon offered us a tour. Although we weren't friends, Karen was familiar to me. We'd been at Girl Scout events together and I often saw airbrushed versions of her around town. Karen owned her own real estate company and pictures of her on grocery store leaflets, SPONSORED BY notices, and FOR SALE signs blanketed our village. In real life, she had sharp features accentuated by short styled hair; for the party she sported low pumps, designer jeans, and a light sweater.

The 9,000-square-foot villa, she told us as we walked from the vestibule to the open-concept kitchen, had been custom-built to her specifications. I thought about all the expensive homes she had shown, memorizing room designs, noting the best decorating plans, filing away desires until she could make them all her own.

Here, in her private golf-course community, she had clearly incorporated everything she'd seen. There were three floors and a lower level that housed a walk-in, climate-controlled wine cellar. At no time was this area referred to as a basement. We looked at the brushed steel, sleek handled, fingerprint-free kitchen appliances (European, we were informed) and then ascended the central staircase to learn about the three hardwoods incorporated into its design.

A greenhouse for Karen's plant-loving husband dominated the third floor. I missed other details as

I became distracted speculating about the weight of dirt brought to a third floor, and why a hothouse wouldn't be on the first floor. I was afraid to ask. I couldn't decide if the question was too personal or too naïve. And I couldn't decide if the other parents—one man rubbed his hand along a banister, commenting on the scrollwork, another inquired about the builder—led lives in which this was common knowledge, this answer to why a greenhouse on the third floor made sense. Or if they were just as confused as me, stretching for comments to link them to this lifestyle, to make them belong.

We continued outside to a brick patio with a heated surface large enough for two sets of outdoor furniture. "Just think, no snow or ice out here," Karen said steering us back inside through a different door.

We wound our way past various bedrooms to Jessica's room where the kids now gathered, sprawled across couches or on the king-sized bed watching music videos on the large-screen television. Jessica didn't complain when her mother guided us into her walk-in closet complete with a dresser and its own TV.

Although my body moved along with the group, I missed a lot of the tour. All the chances to memorize the floor layout, furniture groupings, or color schemes (golds and browns possibly, maybe a forest green) were lost on me. As is too often true, I retreated to the inside of my head. This time stuck overly long on questions about the hothouse's location, the correct word for *basement*, and whether I was the only one who didn't belong here, the only one who didn't know the language for Sub Zero appliances, reliable contractors, or why three hardwoods and their particular combination in whatever pattern we oohed over were better than two or four or one.

I nodded away at our hostess as we toured the third floor of her McMansion in The Legends of Brandybrook. In my mid-forties, reasonably happy at my job as a school social worker, married, and raising fine girls, I was keeping the wrinkles at bay and staying in decent shape. Still, I feared I was just a taller version of my childhood south side of Milwaukee self, worried about fitting in, whether I was wearing the wrong clothes, and whether my questions were stupid—because, despite what teachers said, there were, indeed, stupid questions.

The word *impress* materialized unplanned and unwanted. Different, more shameful even than admitting I wanted to fit in. This wish to belong implied a lack of self-esteem or self-confidence I could work with, but the desire to impress this other mom with her multiple hardwoods was nauseating.

What I wanted—I can accept the immaturity of this—was to be outside it all, to be amused and somewhat proud of my high-water sweatpants and raggedy t-shirt. Or, even better, not to care that this difference in clothing might be judged. Especially when Polly, closing the car door after we'd left, turned to me and asked, "Did you really have to wear that?"

I chuckled at her question, but in truth I would have worn other clothes and thrown on some makeup if I had realized I'd be inside. I had a longing to belong to this club, this higher social stratum which knew the right things to do, the right ways to behave— what gift to get the Girl Scout leader, where to go on spring break. Secret codes recognized by those who took tennis lessons while the kids were at school and then passed the wisdom down to their children. My concern was that I'd paid the price of admission to this community without understanding all the supplementary costs. With this recognition came a memory from deep in my own adolescence, from my high school days.

***

I hadn't seen Catholic girl's school coming following graduation from eighth grade at Saint Gregory the Great. I assumed I'd attend the local public school. However, my parents were separated, and in a move that infuriated me, my mother made private-school tuition part of the divorce stipulation. My father paid the fees, but no one thought about the extras. My class of family—Dad was a laborer, Mom got a factory job after he left— never considered the costs beyond tuition and the compulsory blue and gray uniform skirt.

Successful assimilation, however, required money spent beyond the basics. For example, there'd been the optional blazer. In my family, optional meant unnecessary, but the girls who fit in not only owned those tailored jackets, they knew what days to wear them. They had well-cut blouses from the uniform store instead of from the sale rack at Kmart or, even worse, a cousin's hand-me-downs. They had blue knee socks that didn't slip down to their ankles. My socks, purchased from the discount store, featured loose elastic—broken white threads showing through the dark-colored cuffs. I countered by wearing brown socks left over from my elementary school uniform, purposely pushing at least one to an ankle. When the hem of my skirt ripped along one side, I wore it half-hanging down until I received detention. If I couldn't be in the system, I'd do what I could to be outside of it. That suited me fine. I had close friendships and occasional boyfriends from the Catholic boys' school. I enjoyed a certain reputation as a troublemaker. Nothing that would have gotten me noticed at the public school, but enough cut classes, back talk, and rule infractions to stand out to the nuns of St. Mary's Academy. My goal had been attention, not notoriety. I leaned close to notoriety though, hanging with the smokers in the mornings before school, attending math class under the influence of chemical enhancements, even being arrested during my senior year for underage drinking in a bar. That arrest particularly painful as I was a regular and worried about what the owner and other bartenders would think of me.

I've told my girls little of my teenage life. They seem to think their father and I arrived in this community and our current home without a past. That's fine. Better that than their viewing me as needy or unpopular, as insecure as I really once was.

***

Polly stayed quiet on the drive home, and I mulled over what I'd seen and heard, curious about the day-to-day operations of such a big place. How did they find enough stuff to fill it? Who did the dusting? What were the sounds? Was there a rhythm to the day punctuated by the furnace turning on and off, footsteps across the floor, the toilet flushing, the dresser drawer opening? In our 1,500-square-foot Colonial home—at least a third bigger than where I grew up—we heard each other throughout the evening.

There were the calls of "Turn it down!" The shouts and slammed doors of arguing sisters, questions raised from adjoining rooms, soft *goodnights* easily heard from just down the hall. I was curious how the sounds in a Legends of Brandybrook house echoed through unused spaces and traveled down long passageways. Whether the words became distorted and mumbled—easily ignored, or if Jessica's family relied on the intercom system we'd passed during the tour. "Hello, hello?" crackled into room upon room, the caller leaning against the perfect wall, waiting for an answer.

I fretted about what Polly was thinking. If she contrasted Jessica's room with her own ten-foot-square bedroom, with its small closet and twin bed. Of course. Of course she did. I wanted the view from her bedroom window to mean something to her. Wanted to point out how she could lie in her bed, a captain's bed piled with pillows, look out over the yard and trees and see into the small wooded area leading up the hill to the highway. The string of car lights at all hours of the night a constant metaphor to dream of more, to keep her possibilities open. Perhaps that was just my take on the headlights the evenings I checked on her before I went to sleep. She may have given those cars no more weight than the apple trees, or the fence, or the slight slope to the yard that made it perfect for sledding down with the neighbor kids.

***

Polly was sitting in the hallway outside her bedroom when I came up the stairs after locking up—something she'd never done before. I joined her, our backs up against the white walls, a little of the old beige showing through the current coat of paint in spots. My husband had recently refinished the baseboards to an oaky color, replacing the original walnut popular in the eighties. The carpet was a Berber, put in the summer Polly was born. A light color we shouldn't have picked, it now looked gray despite the cleaning my husband frequently gave it with the Rug Doctor wet-vac machine rented from the Piggly Wiggly.

We sat stunned by all we'd seen, the emotions difficult to name. Jealousy the most obvious as I glanced around the slim, barely fifteen-foot hallway, all three bedroom doors opening off of it, four doors if you included the bathroom. Our loved ones slept a few feet away, unaware of the journey we'd taken. I heard my youngest's bed creak as she turned over, her sigh inside a dream while she resettled herself. This main artery of our home tiny compared to Jessica's bedroom. The area she called her own larger than what connected our entire household.

"My feet touch the wall," Polly said, beginning to drum her toes against the paint.

"They do," I agreed.

"It's really small in here," she continued. I could think of nothing else to say.

***

I don't mean to imply I'd want Jessica's house. I don't covet her stuff. It's more of a sickened feeling, something not right; all of this for one family of five. I wondered how they kept track of each other in all those rooms, down all the long hallways. What I envied was the effortless awareness of the right gift to bring, the ease of language when discussing good schools, the pediatrician agreed upon, or the correct outfit selected. I envied how they *just knew*.

How—I assume—they didn't measure every word for affect against the reaction of others as I had all my high school years. The memory so easily awakened and spinning through me as I watched my daughter assess our home.

Polly talked about Jessica's room, how some of the girls had gone through her drawers and handled her things with an awe that didn't seem friendly, as if she'd become something strange and unfamiliar. My shoulders relaxed as Polly said this. I'd been anxious that she felt disgusted here in our lesser hallway. That she longed for all Jessica possessed and found her father and me lacking with our regular house in our regular neighborhood. Polly hunched down to crawl her feet further up the wall. She told me that the party was weird, that she wanted the big room and the TV, but got sad after she realized the party was about the house and not her friend. "They kept going through her stuff like she wasn't even there."

Only later, in bed for the night with the house settled and quiet, did I realize my concern for Polly was unnecessary, that it's me continuing to need evidence I fit in, reassurance I belong. I remembered the day we met with the banker, unaware I was pregnant. We qualified for a mortgage considerably larger than the one we needed for our current home but wanted to play it safe. Now I worried my husband and I had chosen wrong. That in marrying each other—both from the same working-class neighborhood in Milwaukee—we had guaranteed that neither of us would ever learn how to blend into this community we had moved up to. That, same as my parents, I had incorrectly assumed the basics were good enough and didn't understand about the blazer. Didn't understand about what else needed to be spent.

Hangers

Peggy from up the block is sorting hangers when I call. She's been readying her mother's house for an estate sale since increasing forgetfulness and a bad fall resulted in a nursing home admission for her mom, Bev. The hangers clank against each other as Peggy organizes.

"Do you need any?" she asks me.

Peggy cares about such things despite the chaos of helping Bev settle in. They are close—much closer than my parents and I ever were—and Peggy will make sure each detail is lovingly managed, that even the hangers are handled carefully. I performed these same tasks for my mother two years earlier. When Peggy called to lend support back then, I shared stories of her unkempt home: hidden beer cans, fetid laundry, and unopened bills. I confessed anxiety about finances, guilt over selling my mother's house, and my fear she'd magically recover from alcohol-induced dementia and return to find strangers in her kitchen.

Now it's Peggy's turn. At some point during our conversation, she quiets her hands as I stop hearing the clink of dry cleaners' metal hangers and the dull plastic clack of store-bought ones. Our approaches to undoing our mothers' homes differ—Peggy has lined her own hallways with boxes to look through, something I had never considered. I'm envious of this desire to linger over possessions, even now recognizing my old longing for someone else's mother.

When I began cleaning, I took coats and dresses—some new—to the Salvation Army drop box. My car reeked of mildew after these trips, and I worried about ruining the other accumulated donations. Peggy might have washed the remaining clothing, but I threw it all into the twenty-two-foot dumpster I'd rented. The hangers ended up there also—wooden for pants, plastic for blouses, and pink-knitted for sweaters. I flung them over the dumpster's eight-foot wall, the metal ones gleaming against the fall sky and then clattering down amongst the other garbage.

This was the best I could do when it was my turn to organize, ready the house for a realtor, and find money to pay the nursing home. Or at least it's what I did. The truth is: I didn't want my mother's hangers mixed with my own. Her years of drinking and neglect clung to everything.

Occasional gifts arose from the work, however. While cleaning one afternoon, a memory returned. When I was little, before my parents divorced, Mom ironed in our basement. She'd pull my father's freshly laundered shirts off of hangers hung on the hot water pipes of the ceiling and press them while talking on the phone, the receiver cradled between her neck and shoulder. *General Hospital* played on the TV as she flattened seams and chatted. Once finished, she'd button the warm shirts onto hangers balanced on the ironing board. My job was to carry the shirts upstairs and put them away without wrinkling them. "Don't do a job unless you're going to do it right," she'd say as I started up the stairs.

In between my dismantling of her home and her passing were long days of decline for my mother. Days in which she became her best self, a tender woman who'd kiss me and call me "lovely." Towards the end, when she was unable to do anything for herself, I soaked a mouth swab in Pepsi and held it to her dry lips. When she locked her teeth around it, I talked quietly to her, gently wiggled the swab free, dipped it back in the soda, and pressed it again to her waiting tongue. This small communion between us was slow work, this giving of what she wanted in her drab room, surrounded by her few remaining possessions.

She Wouldn't Rule Anything Out

Lizzy's regression began several months ago. Gently enough. There was additional clumsiness—spilled milk, dropped phones, that kind of thing. She tripped and stumbled over her growing feet and needed reminders to tie her shoes. One day she talked of nothing but a friend's promise to buy her a *Little Mermaid* keychain for her birthday. In general, Lizzy acted more like a tall three-year-old than someone about to turn fifteen.

A cloak of moodiness settled over her. She'd gaze into the distance and look startled when we called her name, put her head down on the table, and complain she was tired. She sighed frequently. Then some sassiness, some good old-fashioned back talk ("I just told you!" "Nobody does it that way." "Why do you always say that?"), appeared at the dinner table. Next, in the blink of an eye, our fine times with this easy child came to a halt. She closed up her face, squinted her eyes, and refused to respond to questions with more than one syllable.

Puberty was upon us.

I wanted to put yellow caution tape around the house, warn visitors to stay away. I considered renting my own apartment. The irony of her starting puberty as I became menopausal was marginally humorous to me—oddly, it was not at all comical to my husband.

"I don't think I can do this," he moaned one night after a particularly tense meal punctuated by Lizzy's desire to text during supper and my loud insistence on conversation.

"How long can it last?" was the most hopeful reply I could give.

***

Polly, our other daughter, had gone off to college earlier in the year. She now lived in a dorm two hours from home. Polly had been a challenging teen—she'd told lies about where she was going, hung out with questionable characters, and let her grades drop into the summer-school range. I was ready for peace and quiet, not another go-round through the drama of adolescence with all its raised voices and demands for equity.

We muddled through. Mostly I remained imperturbable and saint-like in my patience with Lizzy—although occasionally I lost it and hollered, "I'm not putting up with this crap!" I caught myself humming *The Rolling Stones'* "Mother's Little Helper" with a frightening frequency and longingly eyed the liquor aisle of the Piggly Wiggly as I shuffled past with my cart load of family food.

***

One blessed morning before school, Lizzy announced there was blood in her underwear.

Praise be.

Before I left for work, I searched the house for maxi pads—I hadn't been using those products much, and the college kid tended to abscond with any items left unsecured. I found a total of three after rummaging through travel bags and searching underneath a car seat.

Handing the pads to her, I tried to recall what I had said to Lizzy's sister about all of this. I asked, "Does anything feel odd?"

"Odd? Odd like what?"

"Like cramps or your head hurting?"

"Well, I have been kinda moody lately."

Ah. My moment to rise up with a sympathetic hug of a statement, or blow it all with sarcasm. I opted for putting my coat on while mumbling, "I'll say." Then I added: "At least we know you're not psychotic."

Lizzy turned and replied pleasantly, "I wouldn't rule anything out."

We left for work and school. Despite my worry about cramps, feminine hygiene products, and hormone-induced psychosis, everything went fine. At home, the crankiness eased up a moderate percentage.

Then the silliness started. I don't mean just a little immaturity. I mean a full-out return to toddler-hood. There was a constant need for attention, help requested in all areas, even her communication style changed. Lizzy's voice became louder. She called me "Mommy." She repeated it frequently. "Mommy, will you take me out for breakfast?"

"No."

"Mommy, will you make me pancakes?"

"No."

Pause.

"Mommy?"

"Now what?"

"Will you take me out for breakfast?"

I wanted to be kind. I wanted to appreciate her gentle unfolding to the glories of womanhood. Oh, how much nicer this was than the constant challenge my eldest presented! I wanted to enjoy how sweetly she said "Mommy." Mostly I wanted to smack her.

I complained to my husband. He laughed the day I told him Lizzy had reverted to asking "Why" questions. Not the expected adolescent demand, "Why can't I?" but more a replay of the toddler classics:

"Why is that car parked outside?"

"The neighbors have company."

"Why are we having spaghetti for supper?"

"Because."

"Why do they have company?"

My husband chuckled, but I watched his irritation grow with her incessant absentmindedness and dinnertime spills.

We had assumed—quite happily—that we were well past the days of such attentive parenting. Our good intentions about calmly enjoying this colt of a daughter began to fade. I became frustrated with the way she rubbed my head every time she walked past and found myself encouraging sleepovers at the homes of friends.

One night at supper, Lizzy knocked her silverware to the floor while reaching for an orange slice from the bowl on the table. My husband and I rolled our eyes at each other. I gave him my exasperated look, and he raised his brows and tightened his lips. Lizzy reached down to get the cutlery away from the dogs. All was quiet for a moment before she straightened up and turned to look at us with delight in her eyes and a big orange peel quarter smile in her mouth.

Her dad and I laughed then, not even caring that the dogs had wandered off with our flatware. We remembered how fortunate our complaints were, how lucky we were to have this goofy kid taking us down the hormonal path once again.

Heaven's Son
with a Siren

The police officer told me I was a good person. This made me happy. Independent confirmation of decency is always a blessing. Even though I ended up with a speeding ticket, I wanted to hurry home and share the news with anyone who would listen. I am a good person! Shout those joyous words! Unfortunately, there was a bit more. His complete, unedited homily of "You're a good person. You just need to slow down," became my unseen passenger for miles.

Unbeknownst to the Elm Grove police officer who pulled me over on Pilgrim Parkway for going 49 in a 35-mph zone, I had been obsessing about the need to slow down, to quit doing so much for weeks. In fact, I'd only taken the parkway to my psychotherapy practice so I could stop at Ottawa University and pick up handouts for a social work class I was to start teaching in a few days.

Seeing clients two days a week wasn't overwhelming per se, however, I also supervised practicum students and had started taking classes again myself. Added to general home and life maintenance, the Ottawa gig felt like it was tipping the scale right off the mountaintop. The problem was I enjoyed it all: work, teaching, even the endless graduate program demands. But each night, I sat at my kitchen table and repeatedly counted the hours every activity took, trying to refigure how to make it all fit.

Then came the traffic stop for speeding. The policeman stationed himself near the van's window, just behind my shoulder, so that I had to turn to face him. He seemed about my age, fifty, with the ramrod-straight bearing of an ex-military guy. He sported a graying buzz cut, mirrored aviator glasses, and a moustache. His face was inscrutable. I saw myself reflected in each lens and noted the bunched skin between my eyebrows, my face worried and doubled.

And what of his assessment? Did he dismiss me with a mere cataloging of attributes—blue eyes, blonde hair, middle-aged—or did he read more in the way I leaned on the rolled-down window? Some tension in the turn of my shoulders perhaps or a certain look in my eyes that inspired him to offer more? Is this why he had said such a peculiar thing? This declaration of my worth and his judgment regarding the rest of my life. At any rate, I followed his advice and responded to his no-nonsense manner with no-nonsense actions. I thanked him. Drove the rest of the way to work at a prudent speed, and told my employer I needed to reduce my hours. I was moving too fast, doing too much, and needed to slow down. It was only as she nodded and began shuffling papers on her desk that I recognized a desire to leave my job completely. As if the speeding ticket in my purse was a portal to an unimagined life—a portal I wasn't ready for as I'd never left a job for desire alone. I'd always gone onto something else, adding more responsibility, more titles. With busyness, I seemed to believe, I increased the odds I wouldn't become my nervous, addicted mother. But there's more. With busyness and its raft of shoulds, I didn't have to consider how much I might be like my father. My father who let himself follow desire, who let himself leave.

***

What I didn't tell my boss was my suspicion that the police officer might be Jesus. Heaven's son with a siren, pulling me over to deliver his opinion on how I'm doing. Jesus making himself manifest in the everydayness of my life.

Nor did I mention this notion to anyone else at my secular mental health clinic. Even my fellow Unitarian Universalists might have labeled it strange. Most UU's revere Jesus as a good guy and wise teacher; some acknowledge him as the incarnate son of God. Few, however, picture him sporting a badge and mirrored shades. Catholics, the religious troop I grew up in, would certainly struggle with this revised version of Jesus—the holy son on the cross now reduced to a highly personal god delivering blunt messages to his speeding faithful.

I'd been daydreaming when I saw the thirty-five-miles-per-hour sign, realized I was doing closer to fifty-five, hit the brake, and discovered the squad car behind me. Never one to plead or to cry to avoid a ticket—I harbored irrational fears of punishment for any number of venial transgressions—I answered each question carefully and tried to be polite.

The officer, this individualized savior, had been all business when he came to the window. He'd introduced himself and asked, "Do you have a lawful reason for going seventeen miles over the speed limit today?"

I'd started to explain and then interrupted myself to question, "Are there any lawful reasons to go seventeen miles over the speed limit?" He'd paused, and without removing his glasses, smiling, or shifting his features in any way slowly answered, "Well, no, there aren't any. Not really."

His pause was our only personal moment, and it didn't affect the outcome. The officer took my insurance card and driver's license back to his squad car while the multitudes drove past—maybe feeling sorry for me, maybe giving God a shout-out as they checked their own speedometers. Soon he returned with the speeding ticket, his odd blessing, and his counsel for better time and life management.

I slowly reentered the long line of traffic on Pilgrim Parkway. Lights of blue and red swirled above my officer's still-parked squad, the windshield sparkled in the glare of the sun, and I pictured him bent over his clipboard, sunglasses tossed to the side, finishing his paperwork. I had what I needed. Although what I wished—at midlife—was that I didn't find it necessary to have some stand-in deity confirm my choices and hand down approval.

I knew my officer would complete his tasks, sign his name to the forms, and merge back into traffic. Soon he'd pull over someone else who'd reflect in those mirrored shades of his. They'd hear what they needed to hear, nod an understanding to each question, and check their blind spot before driving away, before deciding how to tell the story.

On Coming Home from the Conference

I came home from the conference buoyed by the breakout sessions, refreshed by time with friends, and packing plenty of convention hall swag. My flight came in early, my luggage arrived safely, and my husband, Bruce, picked me up outside the airport as planned.

The house sparkled and smelled of Pine-Sol when I walked in. I was glad to be home in my familiar, predictable place of spouse, kids, and dogs—and grateful for my better half, a guy who enjoys cleaning and takes good care of the family.

After I unpacked, I headed into the upstairs bathroom and discovered a new ruby-colored curtain adorning the window that overlooks our backyard. I called to Bruce, "It's okay, but it sure cuts off the view."

"We can take it down."

"No, no, it's fine."

In the shower, washing the travel away and returning to myself as wife and mom, I noticed a new body wash. Dial for Men. It sported an attractive red and gold label featuring the word "Magnetic" and, in block uppercase letters, the tag: ATTRACTION-ENHANCING. Underneath this, also in block upper-case, but penetrated by a strip of manly blue, the phrase: PHEROMONE-INFUSED. What, you might ask yourself—as I did, while working my own mild-mannered shampoo into my hair—is a contented husband doing with body wash labeled "pheromone-infused?" And, you might wonder—again, as I did by the time I moved onto conditioner—exactly what pheromone-infused means. I thought pheromones were naturally occurring chemicals that made the person across the room hot for you so long as you were single and unattached, but then withered away once you became happily married.

I recognized, with the sixth sense borne of my many years as a social worker, that I was avoiding any cognitive or emotional examination of the phrase "attraction-enhancing." It crossed my mind that product placement in such a highly trafficked area—used by daughters, guests, and me—implied a certain innocence or obliviousness. However, it could also suggest an initial, subconscious inkling of dissatisfaction in what had seemed, only moments earlier, a solid marriage.

In fact, toweling off, I pictured myself typing these very words on some future tearful morning, alone but for a lukewarm cup of coffee, relating how I missed the first signs of trouble, let my attention waver, and paid the price—the children only visiting, the dogs forlorn, and the house for sale. Bruce now with a woman more appreciative of his window treatments, one who would recognize the time spent shopping for drapery, who would remark on how nicely the pleats hung or how the color complemented the tile flooring instead of criticizing.

A woman who would have been home helping instead of off adventuring.

Bruce and our seventeen-year-old daughter, Lizzy, were watching television when I came downstairs. Regretting my negative comments about the new bathroom curtain, I casually asked, "So, what's with the body wash—the pheromone-infused one?"

Lizzy looked up from the TV. "I wondered about that too."

Bruce, from his usual spot on the couch, replied "The Dial? It was on sale. $2.79."

After describing the cost of the other brands, he added, "I don't even know what pheromones are."

I thought this answer came a tad fast. I countered, "Well, you know what 'attraction-enhancing' means."

"I don't think it says that."

At this point, Lizzy—clearly enjoying our exchange—happily ran upstairs for the offending cleanser and rushed back downstairs to read aloud the aforementioned descriptions.

Bruce—wearing a long-sleeved white t-shirt pallid against his winter skin and black shorts with multi-colored socks—refused to understand the implications and suggested there was no need for enhancement as he had always been a "stud muffin." Then he turned his gaze back to the antics on *Storage Wars*.

I couldn't let it go. For the next several mornings I faced the accusatory block letters throbbing against the blue ribbon. I wondered if this was how it happens, small omens laughed off or dismissed in the busyness of work, raising kids, and the sweet complacency of marriage. I couldn't resist googling "pheromones" and found scant evidence to support liquid soap as a sexual attractant. And the body wash's list of ingredients read nearly the same as my shampoo's. Of course, this wasn't the important thing. It's not the reality of the ingredient, but the belief system created. Tell yourself you're more enhancing and the odds are you will be.

That's what I would tell one of my psychotherapy clients anyway—right after gently confronting the insecurity lurking around the edges of the story. At the same time, I might wonder aloud to him or her, "Why all of the concentration on this?"

To switch chairs for a minute and answer my own question—I can feel the blush crawling up my face—aren't I the one with the opportunities? Night after night of post-conference schmoozing and, at the very least, all that elbow rubbing?

It's not only opportunity. It's history. My family includes generations of adventurers and galli-vanters. Heck, both my great-grandfather and father became mid-life runaways, and my maternal grand-father was infamous for a septuagenarian fling with his cousin, Bernice.

It seems my over-concentration on body wash may have been scented with projection.

It's the adventuring I'm attracted to, not some need to stray—a desire, stronger with age, to be off exploring more than at home decorating. It's an itchy feeling of not fitting in when everyone gathers around the TV for the night. With this analysis, I understand that my fears of becoming like my overanxious mother may have kept me from recognizing the more captivating danger—that of my father's wanderlust. A few days later, I mulled over these ideas while pinning back the curtain, the color nice against the woodwork, the window no longer muffled.

"Did you see how I changed the curtain?" I asked Bruce when he hadn't praised my domestic exertion within an hour.

"Yeah, I thought I already said that. You can see the backyard a lot better."

He was right—the view was much improved. The hammock swaying between our two apple trees, the new outdoor furniture on the patio, and the baskets of flowers hanging from the fence were all more inviting without the gauzy material in the way. Too often it was my thoughts I saw when I looked out the window; my focus coming to rest on whatever confirmed the images tumbling around in my head. Or maybe all of those sneaky pheromones caterwauling through the air and just looking for trouble continued to blur my vision. Most days though, the cars that journeyed on the highway visible beyond our backyard caught and held my attention at least as much as the hammock, the planters, and the cushioned deck chairs.

Toto, Where
Have You Gone?

Bruce and I put the Christmas tree up yesterday. It leans left of center in a corner of the living room where an end table usually stands. Mismatched lights, few ornaments, no glitz or glamour. I don't think the tree cares one way or the other, the kids won't notice; and the neighbors, when they come for our annual holiday party, will politely exclaim, "Oh what a beautiful tree!" They'd say the same thing even if we hung old socks on it.

Rituals change through the years. I remember trying to establish what the parenting books call "a beautiful family culture" around the decorating of the tree with Bruce and our two girls. Collecting Christmas decorations and adornments that seemed *just right* became important to me. They needed to be handcrafted and have a noteworthy memory attached, such as the tatted snowflakes my grandmother made, painted ceramic Santas given by a special friend, or stained-glass icicles from an art fair. I also began buying a special ornament every year for each girl. Decorations they'd eventually want to take along to their own homes and hang on their own trees, while happily reminiscing about loving times spent with family.

I bought a sheep the year the baby learned to say "baa," a cow when the eldest had a livestock fascination, and nutcrackers the year we all dressed up to see the ballet performed downtown. We have a flute from the years of Polly's lessons, and a duck from the single year Lizzy played trumpet. Then there's the Toto ornament celebrating Lizzy's starring role in *The Wizard of Oz*. I spent weeks looking for Toto, at last finding it online for $25. Once it arrived, I discovered how very small it was, not more than an inch from nose to tail. We lost poor Toto within two years and Lizzy hasn't ever missed him—although I've always held out hope for his miraculous return from some long-forgotten stash of Christmas trimmings.

During the preschool and elementary years, we added decorations the girls made at school: cardboard wreaths and pipe-cleaner candy canes identical to the ones I made thirty years earlier. We hung them until they fell apart or got tossed by the maker who could no longer abide the embarrassment of geeky class pictures glued inside a multitude of holiday shapes.

Those elementary-school years were the best ones for tree decorating as a family. I could control the activity, tell everyone they loved doing this—and the girls, if they didn't look up to see my husband roll his eyes, believed me. In those days, they'd pause over many of the ornaments, say something about when we got it, remember if it was their special one from a past holiday, peer into the tree to see if they could find a favorite, and even ask permission to take a candy cane from the tree.

During middle school and high school, the girls' friends came over on tree-trimming night. My eldest, Polly, never did anything without a pack. And those were good years, too. The kids decorating the tree all helter skelterish, laughing and telling stories of their own families. All the candy canes disappearing before they got anywhere near the tree, Lizzy trying to fit in, Bruce hauling items down from the attic, me making cup after cup of hot chocolate, and the dogs barking at all the commotion.

Now Polly is in college and hasn't helped decorate the tree for what feels like ages. The last couple of years of high school, she sprawled on the couch and complained continually, begging for release while the rest of us hung the ornaments. Lizzy, trying to keep peace in the family, remained polite and helpful but sighed often. My husband watched football with decorations in his hand, putting them on the tree only when nudged and directed.

***

Then this year, while we're driving fifteen-year-old Lizzy over to a friend's house, Bruce suggests we "get the tree done."

"Well, it's a good night for it, but Lizzy won't be there," I reply. There is silence from the backseat until Bruce cuts his eyes to the rearview mirror and begins to laugh.

"That's okay. Really, it's okay," Lizzy says. Bruce tells me her face is lit up with joy and she's bouncing in her seat. I tsk and agree we can do the tree without her.

We discuss the idea of forgoing the tree completely next year as we drive through the dark to the friend's house, weighing the pros: less mess and work (Bruce), and the cons: where to put the gifts (Lizzy).

To my surprise, I don't get mad or hurt. I don't shrink up inside the way I might have in the past, thinking the suggestion meant we were a failed family, not able to create what I assumed everyone else in the subdivision had. Maybe, like Bruce and Lizzy, and doubtless—if she were along—Polly, I've also come to a different place as these years have gone on. Ready to have the holiday be about what we want, and not about fixing old wounds or trying to be like everyone else on the block.

***

Bruce and I decorate the tree with only one extra run to Walgreens. Now, thanks to changing technology, we have two different colors of white lights on one small tree; the new-fangled halogen ones we bought on sale and our remaining traditional twinkling bulbs. I shrug my shoulders, unwilling to take off the lights again, to purchase ones that match, and to start over. This, in contrast to all of the years I wrapped white lights around the inside of the tree and strung colored lights on the outer branches. We bring down two of the six boxes of baubles from the attic, and I pick out my favorites to hang on the tree. Bruce tosses crumpled newspaper from the boxes into the garbage. I watch his quick movements and then remind him to shake each piece out just in case something is rolled inside.

Oh Toto, where have you gone?

Afterwards we sit back on the couch, have a glass of wine, gaze at the tree, and decide it's good enough. I miss my grandmother's tatted snowflakes, but I'm not willing to hunt for them in the attic and hang them by myself.

In a burst that startles me, I tell Bruce about the video in my head of all of us looking forward to decorating the tree every year, even Polly making it a point to come home from college when she knows it's tree trimming night. There is popcorn and eggnog. Old Christmas favorites play in the background, someone sings along, there is frequent conversation starting with the word *remember*, and good-hearted teasing about what Santa might put under the tree. An annual evening of family togetherness that nobody wants to miss or ever leave—our foursome strung with tinsel, shimmering in the reflected glow from the tree lights.

Bruce laughs and reminds me of the glow of Lizzy's smile in the rearview mirror when she realized she didn't have to help with the tree. I nod, put the lid on the ornament box, and return it to the attic.

Later, after Bruce has gone to bed, the house has fallen quiet, and only the two dogs are still awake, watching me from their sleepy spots, I'll turn on the Christmas tree lights, gaze through the branches to where the memories still linger, and I'll remember. I'll remember for all of us.

Acknowledgements

Heartfelt thanks to the church ladies for walks, talks, weekends away, and round-the-clock encouragement. Thanks also to the St. Mary's Academy gals (knowledge and virtue united) for continued laughter and memories both old and new. For all at the Bennington Writing Seminars—my term mentors and good friends—your wisdom continues to guide me. Ongoing thanks to the folks of Red Oak Writing, specifically my Moving Pens round table. Your keen comments and insightful questions keep me returning to the page with fresh resolve. And a special shout out to Linda Michel-Cassidy whose discerning eye and perceptive comments have enhanced every step of the manuscript process from early drafts onward.

A memoir, of course, cannot exist without family. I am blessed to have a rich legacy of cousins and aunts, grandparents, parents, and loving big brothers. It's through their guidance and example, as well as the love of my husband and daughters, that I am able to move in the world as I do.

Thank you to all who have shared a story, corrected a version, enriched a telling. I am filled with gratitude for all you have given me.

And lastly, to the kind and patient staff of Vine Leaves Press who—thank goodness—sent a follow-up email that led me to the acceptance letter nestled deep in my spam file. I am forever grateful for your dedication. Your enthusiasm and commitment to the manuscript was evident with every email and with each decision made.

Many thanks to the editors of the following publications in which portions of this book first appeared, sometimes in slightly different versions: *Museum of Americana, Redivider, The Notebook, Riding Light Review, Midwestern Gothic, Auscult, The Peninsula Pulse, Corners: Voices on Change, Family Stories from the Attic, and Orphans: An Anthology of Prose,* as well as recordings for *WUWM's Lake Effect* (Milwaukee's local NPR affiliate).

Vine Leaves Press

Enjoyed this book?
Go to *vineleavespress.com* to find more.

CPSIA information can be obtained
at www.ICGtesting.com
Printed in the USA
BVHW071216280820
587364BV00003B/212

9 781925 965360